118th Open Championship

ROYAL TROON GOLF CLUB
Troon, Scotland
July 20-24, 1989

James E. Dyekman

THE OPEN CHAMPIONSHIP
1989

THE OPEN CHAMPIONSHIP 1989

WRITERS

JOHN HOPKINS
RAYMOND JACOBS
MICHAEL McDONNELL
ALISTER NICOL
MARINO PARASCENZO
MICHAEL WILLIAMS
MARK WILSON

PHOTOGRAPHERS

LAWRENCE LEVY
BRIAN MORGAN

EDITOR

BEV NORWOOD

AUTHORIZED BY THE
CHAMPIONSHIP COMMITTEE
OF THE ROYAL AND ANCIENT
GOLF CLUB OF ST ANDREWS

TRANSWORLD PUBLISHERS LTD
61-63 Uxbridge Road, London W5 5SA

TRANSWORLD PUBLISHERS (AUSTRALIA) PTY LTD
15-23 Helles Avenue, Moorebank, NSW 2170

TRANSWORLD PUBLISHERS (NZ) LTD
Cnr Moselle and Waipareira Aves,
Henderson, Auckland

Published 1989 by Partridge Press
a division of Transworld Publishers Ltd
Copyright © 1989 The Championship Committee Merchandising
Limited

Statistics of 118th Open Championship produced on a
Unisys Computer System.
Designed by Graham Mitchener.

British Library Cataloguing in Publication Data
The Open Championship 1989
1. Great Britain. Golf. Competitions. British Open
Golf Championship.
796.352'73'0941
ISBN 185225–0992

Printed in Great Britain
by Richard Clay

CONTENTS

THE
CHAMPIONSHIP
COMMITTEE

CHAIRMAN

G. M. SIMMERS, OBE

DEPUTY CHAIRMAN

T. B. TAYLOR

COMMITTEE

H. M. CAMPBELL
J. C. DAWSON
R. FOSTER
P. W. J. GREENHOUGH
R. D. MUCKHART JR.
DR D. W. NISBET
D. I. PEPPER
W. G. N. ROACH
P. G. SHILLINGTON
J. K. TATE

BUSINESS MEMBER

N. J. CRICHTON

ADDITIONAL MEMBER

D. REA O'KELLY
COUNCIL OF NATIONAL GOLF UNIONS

CO-OPTED MEMBER

J. A. GRAY
P. G. A. EUROPEAN TOUR

SECRETARY

M. F. BONALLACK, OBE

DEPUTY SECRETARY

W. G. WILSON

CHAMPIONSHIP SECRETARY

D. HILL

ASSISTANT SECRETARY (CHAMPIONSHIPS)

D. R. WEIR

INTRODUCTION

BY G.M. SIMMERS
Chairman of Championship Committee
Royal and Ancient Golf Club of St Andrews

The sun shone all week on the true links course of Royal Troon and the 118th Open Championship provided the large crowds with one of the most exciting finishes ever seen.

An amazing round of 64 by Greg Norman was to be the prelude to the first four-hole play-off and the first three-man play-off in the history of the Open. My congratulations to Mark Calcavecchia for his thoroughly deserved victory, but spare a thought for Greg Norman and Wayne Grady, who also contributed so superbly to such a memorable conclusion.

The Championship Committee of the Royal and Ancient Golf Club is pleased to present this official annual and I hope that it will bring back outstanding memories to all our spectators and literally thousands of volunteers who assisted us during the week.

Finally, as always, I would like to thank all our contributors and photographers, all experts in their fields, for their efforts in providing us with this lasting record of the 1989 Open Championship and I hope it will be a fitting tribute to the members of Royal Troon Golf Club, who so graciously allowed us the courtesy of their course.

G.M. Simmers, OBE

FOREWORD

BY MARK CALCAVECCHIA

It should come as no surprise that the past several weeks have been the happiest of my life. Within the brief span of seventeen days were two events to cherish for a lifetime: winning the major championship and then, far more importantly, becoming a father for the first time. My wife, Sheryl, gave birth to our daughter, Britney Jo, on 8 August.

I am pleased to have had the opportunity to write this foreword, not only for the obvious reason that I am the British Open champion, but also because it gives me an opportunity to thank again everyone responsible for organizing that great championship.

As I said at Royal Troon, for me to win took the best golf I could play and a couple of miracles from God. Everything seemed to go my way when I needed it most. It often seems to happen that way, when it's someone's turn to win.

Things were happening so quickly, my mind is still a bit fuzzy about some of the details. I'm sure going to enjoy reading this book, to remember those times and to share the memories with Sheryl and, in several years, Britney Jo.

Mark Calcavecchia

118TH OPEN CHAMPIONSHIP

* Denotes amateurs

NAME	SCORES				TOTAL	MONEY
Mark Calcavecchia, USA	71	68	68	68	275	£80,000
Greg Norman, Australia	69	70	72	64	275	55,000
Wayne Grady, Australia	68	67	69	71	275	55,000
PLAY-OFF:						
Calcavecchia	4	3	3	3		
Norman	3	3	4	x		
Grady	4	4	4	4		
Tom Watson, USA	69	68	68	72	277	40,000
Jodie Mudd, USA	73	67	68	70	278	30,000
David Feherty, N. Ireland	71	67	69	72	279	26,000
Fred Couples, USA	68	71	68	72	279	26,000
Eduardo Romero, Argentina	68	70	75	67	280	21,000
Paul Azinger, USA	68	73	67	72	280	21,000
Payne Stewart, USA	72	65	69	74	280	21,000
Mark McNulty, Zimbabwe	75	70	70	66	281	17,000
Nick Faldo, England	71	71	70	69	281	17,000
Howard Clark, England	72	68	72	70	282	13,000
Philip Walton, Ireland	69	74	69	70	282	13,000
Craig Stadler, USA	73	69	69	71	282	13,000
Roger Chapman, England	76	68	67	71	282	13,000
Mark James, England	69	70	71	72	282	13,000
Steve Pate, USA	69	70	70	73	282	13,000
Derrick Cooper, England	69	70	76	68	283	8,575
Don Pooley, USA	73	70	69	71	283	8,575
Tom Kite, USA	70	74	67	72	283	8,575
Larry Mize, USA	71	74	66	72	283	8,575
Davis Love III, USA	72	70	73	69	284	6,733
Vijay Singh, Fiji	71	73	69	71	284	6,733
Jose-Maria Olazabal, Spain	68	72	69	75	284	6,733
Chip Beck, USA	75	69	68	73	285	5,800
Stephen Bennett, England	75	69	68	73	285	5,800
Scott Simpson, USA	73	66	72	74	285	5,800
Lanny Wadkins, USA	72	70	69	74	285	5,800
Gary Koch, USA	72	71	74	69	286	4,711
Brian Marchbank, Scotland	69	74	73	70	286	4,711
Jack Nicklaus, USA	74	71	71	70	286	4,711
Peter Jacobsen, USA	71	74	71	70	286	4,711
Miguel Martin, Spain	68	73	73	72	286	4,711
Masashi Ozaki, Japan	71	73	70	72	286	4,711
Mark Davis, England	77	68	67	74	286	4,711
Ian Baker-Finch, Australia	72	69	70	75	286	4,711
Jeff Hawkes, South Africa	75	67	69	75	286	4,711
Jeffrey Woodland, Australia	74	67	75	71	287	4,100
Michael Harwood, Australia	71	72	72	72	287	4,100
Tommy Armour III, USA	70	71	72	74	287	4,100
Jose Rivero, Spain	71	75	72	70	288	3,725
Mark O'Meara, USA	72	74	69	73	288	3,725
Lee Trevino, USA	68	73	73	74	288	3,725
Raymond Floyd, USA	73	68	73	74	288	3,725
Sandy Lyle, Scotland	73	73	71	72	289	3,550
Naomichi Ozaki, Japan	71	71	69	78	289	3,550
Mark McCumber, USA	71	68	70	80	289	3,550
Ian Woosnam, Wales	74	72	73	71	290	3,400
Johnny Miller, USA	72	69	76	73	290	3,400
Christy O'Connor Jr, Ireland	71	73	72	74	290	3,400

Player						
Brett Ogle, Australia	74	70	76	71	291	3,100
Ben Crenshaw, USA	73	73	74	71	291	3,100
Tateo Ozaki, Japan	75	71	73	72	291	3,100
Mark Roe, England	74	71	73	73	291	3,100
Michael Allen, USA	74	67	76	74	291	3,100
Emmanuel Dussart, France	76	68	73	74	291	3,100
Tony Johnstone, Zimbabwe	71	71	74	75	291	3,100
Richard Boxall, England	74	68	73	76	291	3,100
Gene Sauers, USA	70	73	72	76	291	3,100
Paul Hoad, England	72	71	77	72	292	2,675
Mike Reid, USA	74	72	73	73	292	2,675
Curtis Strange, USA	70	74	74	74	292	2,675
Bob Tway, USA	76	70	71	75	292	2,675
Ronan Rafferty, N. Ireland	70	72	74	76	292	2,675
David Graham, Australia	74	72	69	77	292	2,675
Wayne Stephens, England	66	72	76	78	292	2,675
Ken Green, USA	75	71	68	78	292	2,675
* Russell Claydon, England	70	74	74	75	293	2,425
Luis Carbonetti, Argentina	71	72	74	76	293	2,425
Sandy Stephen, Scotland	71	74	71	77	293	2,425
Colin Gillies, Scotland	72	74	74	74	294	2,400
Brad Faxon, USA	72	72	75	76	295	2,400
Peter Teravainen, USA	72	73	72	78	295	2,400
Emlyn Aubrey, USA	72	73	73	78	296	2,400
Martin Sludds, Ireland	72	74	73	78	297	2,400
* Robert Karlsson, Sweden	75	70	76	78	299	2,400
Seve Ballesteros, Spain	72	73	76	78	299	2,400
Gavin Levenson, South Africa	69	76	77	79	301	2,400
Bernhard Langer, West Germany	71	73	83	82	309	2,400

NON QUALIFIERS AFTER 36 HOLES
(All professionals receive £500)

Player			
Tom Weiskopf, USA	74	73	147
Stephen Field, England	76	71	147
Sam Torrance, Scotland	70	77	147
Nick Price, Zimbabwe	74	73	147
Larry Nelson, USA	73	74	147
Martin Poxon, England	71	76	147
Paul Affleck, England	72	75	147
Stephen Hamill, N. Ireland	74	73	147
Neil Hansen, England	73	74	147
Neal Briggs, England	77	70	147
Bary Lane, England	74	73	147
Peter Senior, Australia	74	73	147
Des Smyth, Ireland	78	69	147
John Bland, South Africa	72	75	147
Bob E. Smith, USA	70	77	147
David Ray, England	73	74	147
Mike Smith, USA	76	71	147
Fuzzy Zoeller, USA	73	75	148
Andy Bean, USA	73	75	148
* Ernie Els, South Africa	72	76	148
Brian Barnes, Scotland	73	75	148
Gordon Brand Jr, Scotland	76	72	148
Michael Clayton, Australia	74	74	148
Paul Mayo, Wales	75	73	148
Charlie Bolling, USA	73	76	149
Peter Baker, England	74	75	149
Wayne Henry, England	76	73	149
Denis Durnian, England	75	74	149
* Gary Evans, England	73	76	149
Steve Jones, USA	73	77	150
Larry Rinker, USA	75	75	150
David Llewellyn, Wales	78	72	150
Jonathan Sewell, England	78	72	150
Gary Emerson, England	75	75	150
Andrew Stubbs, England	72	78	150
Steen Tinning, Denmark	78	72	150
Philip Parkin, Wales	73	77	150
Ross McFarlane, England	73	77	150
Paul Carrigill, England	78	72	150
Anders Sorensen, Denmark	74	76	150
Keith Waters, England	74	76	150
Peter Mitchell, England	75	75	150
Jeff Sluman, USA	78	73	151
Paul Carmen, England	76	75	151
Vicente Fernandez, Argentina	75	76	151
Gordon J. Brand, England	78	73	151
Babe Hiskey, USA	75	77	152
Ken Brown, Scotland	74	78	152
Gary Player, South Africa	79	73	152
David Williams, England	77	75	152
Mark Mouland, Wales	77	75	152
Eamonn Darcy, Ireland	75	77	152
Wayne Riley, Australia	76	77	153
John Price, Australia	80	73	153
Paul Eales, England	74	79	153
Daniel Lozano, Spain	79	74	153
David Frost, South Africa	75	79	154
Chris Moody, England	81	73	154
* Stephen Dodd, Wales	79	75	154
* Gary Milne, England	79	75	154
* Jerome J. Oshea, England	80	75	155
Peter Cowen, England	81	74	155
Philip Harrison, England	79	76	155
* Andrew D. Hare, England	73	82	155
Gordon Townhill, England	79	77	156
Tony Jacklin, England	80	77	157
Rodger Davis, Australia	78	79	157
Paul Kent, England	78	79	157
Paul Broadhurst, England	73	84	157
Nobuo Serizawa, Japan	79	78	157
David J. Russell, England	80	78	158
* James M. Noon, Scotland	81	77	158
Johan Rystrom, Sweden	79	79	158
John Garner, England	78	81	159
* Eric Meeks, USA	81	80	161
Arnold Palmer, USA	82	82	164

ROUND ROYAL TROON

No. 1 364 YARDS, PAR 4

The first three holes are comparatively straightforward, all two-shotters less than 400 yards long. On the first, the golfer must avoid the two left-hand fairway bunkers and the four bunkers around the green.

No. 2 391 YARDS, PAR 4

In a following wind, the three cross bunkers are within range from the tee, and the golfer is best advised to lay up. The pear-shaped green is strategically guarded by three bunkers, but here again is an opportunity for a three.

No. 3 379 YARDS, PAR 4

Downwind, the tee shot must be brought up short of the burn, about 275 yards out, to position the pitch to the kidney-shaped green, which is protected by two bunkers on the left and a third on the right. All three greens on the opening holes have been driven, a gamble unlikely to be taken during an Open Championship.

No. 4 557 YARDS, PAR 5

This is where the course really starts. As Brian Anderson, the host club's professional, says of this and the other long holes, 'More fours will be made if they are played for fives.' The key is the drive, which must avoid the bunker on the inside of the right-curving fairway, but not run into the rough on the far side.

No. 5 210 YARDS, PAR 3

Anderson's advice here applies equally to the three other short holes: 'There is no percentage in hitting the front edges of the greens. Fly the ball to the target with a shot that is always one club, or a half club, more than it looks.'

No. 6 577 YARDS, PAR 5

This is the longest hole in British championship golf. The golfer must skirt the hazards of sand and rough visible from the tee, then Anderson recommends placing the second shot on the flat ground near the left-hand bunker, the ideal spot from which to approach the small green.

No. 7 402 YARDS, PAR 4

The golfer must keep the tee shot on a fairway which is well-bunkered and narrow in the landing area. A solid drive will open the way to an approach to an equally well-defended green, which slopes upward quite sharply from the front.

No. 8 126 YARDS, PAR 3

As Anderson notes, 'The only safe place to miss this green is through it.' The antithesis of the sixth hole, this is the shortest in British championship golf. In the 1973 Open, Gene Sarazen, then aged 71, holed in one, and in two from a bunker. On the other hand, Herman Tissies, a German amateur, took 15 in the 1950 Open Championship.

No. 9 423 YARDS, PAR 4

The prudent method of playing this hole is to lay up short of the left-hand bunkers. This will leave an iron shot of medium range, where the flag will be visible, but not the bottom of the flagstick.

No. 10 438 YARDS, PAR 4

This is the first of Royal Troon's two holes without a bunker.

There is no reason to lay up, so a driver is needed, but there is little margin for error. The golfer goes as far left as his confidence will allow him. Even then, his problems are not over. The green, falling away on both sides, presents an elusive target.

No. 11 481 YARDS, PAR 5

Traditionally, the eleventh has been one of the least amenable holes on the course. The tee shot is at an acute angle, there are whins everywhere, and the railway line follows the hole down the right side. For safety, a one iron might be used from the tee, but that would leave another substantial shot to a green which presents a narrow target between the boundary wall and the hole's only bunker.

No. 12 431 YARDS, PAR 4

The drive is the less demanding shot of the two on this hole. The fairway curves quite gently to the right, but the flagstick is not easy to attack, wherever it is placed on the narrow, two-tiered green, which slopes abruptly down from the back.

No. 13 465 YARDS, PAR 4

This proved to be the most intractable hole in the 1982 Open Championship, and was the start of Nick Price's downfall. Even into a moderate wind, only a long drive will reach the fairway, and a second shot of substance is needed to carry to a raised green between rough sandhills. There are no bunkers; none are needed.

No. 14 179 YARDS, PAR 3

Fully visible from the tee, the pear-shaped green has bunkers guarding the entrance, and there is a steep bank beyond.

No. 15 457 YARDS, PAR 4

The essence in tackling this hole is to hit the longest and straightest drive possible between the fairway bunkers. The second shot is no less demanding, to a sunken and well-protected green. The sure route is the left; the riskier shot needs the help of a kindly bounce down from the bank on the right.

No. 16 542 YARDS, PAR 5

This is a genuine three-shot hole, unless there is a strong following wind. Few will attempt to carry the ditch on the tee shot. The second shot must be held left to open up a long, narrow and heavily-defended green. There is a chance for a birdie, of course, but a par is unlikely to cause a loss of ground.

No. 17 223 YARDS, PAR 3

Whatever the club selection from the tee — anything from a driver to a two iron is possible — the imperative is to hold the green, from whose plateau the ground falls away steeply on the left and towards deep bunkers on the other side.

No. 18 452 YARDS, PAR 4

The eighteenth is the only radically changed hole since the 1982 Open Championship. It was lengthened by 25 yards, and a bunker was added, short of the existing two on the left side. The carry from the tee to the fairway is 225 yards. Although the green is receptive to even a long-iron shot, its defences comprise not only bunkers but also an out-of-bounds path menacingly close between it and the clubhouse.

ROYAL TROON

BY RAYMOND JACOBS

There must be times when the subscription to a club which has custody of one of the outstanding courses of the world seems a high price to pay for membership. The same almost ceaseless tread of visitors' feet which can wear out carpets, rough up greens, and damage the health of fairways with impartial vigour also can subsidize handsomely the members' annual liability. When the club also is regularly on the rota for the Open Championship, blessings can come as well in the agreeable guise of the Royal and Ancient Golf Club's not insubstantial fee for use of the facilities.

The week occupied by the Open each July lasts a long time, five months more or less. The first visible signs of the mid-summer extravaganza emerge in early spring. Construction of the grandstands begins in April. Erection of tentage and score-boards follow, then the electricity, plumbing and communications services move in. Within two weeks of the champion having ecstatically raised aloft the silver claret jug that is the antique symbol of the Open, removal of everything will have been completed except for the stands, whose dismemberment will extend well into August.

Such feats, complications and intrusions, let alone acting as hosts to an Open Championship even in its formative days, could not have entered the fertile imagination of Troon's founding fathers. The Open had been in existence for eighteen years – held for the first twelve years at Prestwick, the inaugurating club on the south side of the Pow Burn, and once more afterwards – before twenty-three pioneers, culled from Troon, other parts of Ayrshire and Glasgow, met at the Portland Arms Hotel in March 1878, to launch what at the time seemed a highly uncertain venture.

Previously, four or five holes had been laid out over a field inland from what was to become the permanent location of the course. The target holes were hacked out of the ground with a table knife. The course which followed was, by all accounts, not that much more sophisticated. Initially, five (soon after six) holes were laid out over the ground which now accommodates the first three and last two and a half holes; in other words, only as far as Gnawys Burn, which intersects the present third and sixteenth fairways. Beyond that, the land towards the Pow Burn was so untamed – 'full of dunes and hillocks, whins, heather, and broom' – that the expense of immediately creating more holes was considered too great. The humble pedigree of the club's beginnings was reflected in the annual subscription of one guinea and in the clubhouse, a disused railway carriage measuring some twenty by fifteen feet. Enthusiasm for the game could not, however, be denied.

By 1883 there were twelve holes, five years later the number was increased to the regulation eighteen, and the growth of the game was such that in 1895 a relief course, the Portland, was built. Advances also had been made on the convenience front. Minutes of a meeting held in 1880 disclose that every consideration was given to 'the propriety of adding to the clubhouse, a lavatory.' By 1886 a proper stone-built clubhouse had been opened, and two years after that a crest also had been devised, five clubs bound by a throng in the shape of a snake and the unimpeachable motto *Tam Arte Quam Marte* (As Much By Skill As By Strength).

Troon was by now ready to accept the status and responsibilities of a championship course. Not for the first time, or the last, the Ladies' Golf Union decided, in advance of their supposedly more perceptive sex, that in 1904 the links were ready for their British championship, and they have returned

on three subsequent occasions. The first of four men's British Amateur championships was held at Troon in 1938 and the first of five Scottish championships in 1923. The first men's quadrangular home international matches were played in 1932, having been upstaged, it goes almost without saying, by the corresponding women's event by all of seven years.

The association between the Open Championship and the course (which in recognition of its centenary year in 1978 was created the first Royal club in the west of Scotland) gave until very recently every sign of ambivalence. Forty-five years after its most humble of beginnings, the championship was first played there in 1923. Before it was to return twenty-seven years had elapsed, another twelve went by until the third occasion, eleven more until the fourth, and nine before the fifth. The 1989 Open was the first to be played on the links in the same decade as its immediate predecessor. These prolonged, if admittedly reducing, intervals offer an odd paradox.

After all, Troon was one of the courses introduced to bring a degree of novelty to the circuit, firmly established over many years, of St Andrews, Muirfield, Hoylake, Royal St George's, and, still, by its next-door neighbour, Prestwick. Reasons for these lengthy intervals, after the initial introduction to the circle in 1923, become all the more strange when, after the notoriously undisciplined crowd scenes of only two years later, together with the cramped layout of its last four holes, Prestwick was removed permanently from the Open list. For more than a quarter of a century, the west of Scotland was left to fret at having been declared an exclusion zone.

There were, certainly, difficulties – of traffic flow, crowd control and space – but none which could not equally be laid against other established courses on the rota. As Prestwick Airport traffic developed, low-flying aircraft over the course did present a unique problem and led later to the barbed remark, 'You can tell he's a Troon member, He's stone deaf and his clothes reek of kerosene.' The nature of the links tended not to be treated very sympathetically. Its character was defined, politely, as rugged; Muirfield's was fair, Carnoustie's unyielding, and

Turnberry's spectacular. St Andrews was just its gloriously eccentric self.

Even in 1923 the choice of Troon was rather forced on the R & A. Reconstruction work was taking place at Muirfield, the original choice, but Troon itself was not exactly short of alterations, which went a good deal further than skin deep. James Braid, whose design commitments must surely have obliged him to spend more time on trains travelling between projects than any course architect before or since, tightened up the target areas to the extent of introducing some forty bunkers, and he altered the fifth from a dog-leg par four to become the first of four short holes as different in character as they are comparably testing.

The configuration is in the established links tradition – six holes straight out, six in an anticlockwise buttonhook, and six holes straight in. Depending on the strength and direction of the wind, an imbalance becomes inevitable. Sixty-six years ago, Arthur Havers responded best. As a sixteen-year-old he had qualified for the last championship before the First World War and in 1922 finished fourth. Over the course, then 6,583 yards long, Havers, now aged twenty-six, added a 76 to three 73s for a total of 295, to beat the holder, Walter Hagen, by a stroke. It was to be the last British victory for eleven years, until 1934, when Henry Cotton won at Royal St George's.

That Open was marked by two other exceptional episodes. Gene Sarazen, the reigning US Open champion, ran into dreadful weather in the second round of the qualifying competition, then compulsory for all, and failed to survive. (Some amends were made exactly fifty years later, when Sarazen holed in one at the Postage Stamp, the short eighth, in the first round of the 1973 Open and holed a bunker recovery for a two there the next day.) Before that misfortune, the iron clubs of the American professionals were banned because protruding ragged pieces of metal, it was claimed, allowed excessive backspin to be imparted to the ball. Recent dissensions suggest that, once again, the more things change, the more they remain the same. In the event, a call was sent out to local shipyards and joiners for rasps and files to reduce the clubfaces to an acceptable level of smoothness.

In those days, almost in golf's pre-history as they seem now, a player won the Open and that was that. The prize money was negligible and there were no great fringe benefits, such as the appearance money, equipment and clothing contracts, company days, and so on that are part of the contemporary victors' expected spoils. Those lucrative days were still over the horizon in 1950 when the championship returned to Troon. Bobby Locke successfully defended the title he was to win twice more. The accommodating condition of the links, still a modest 6,583 yards, and the improved standard of play and of clubs and balls unleashed scoring forces of unprecedented strength.

Locke, as portly and prepossessing as a Wodehouse butler, had a two-stroke victory with his total of 279, the first below 280 in the history of the championship. The weather, though, was not hostile and the course not only played shorter than its already exiguous length, but had greens more heavily watered than was considered appropriate for a links. Locke feigned reluctance even to walk onto the greens in his first practice round, saying, 'They're like carpets.' When the Australian, Norman von Nida, learned that the greens would continue to be watered, he bet on the South African, one of the greatest putters the game has known, to win, with the verdict, 'The championship is being handed to Locke on a plate.' The state of the course also meant that the thirty-five players who qualified for the final thirty-six holes all broke 300; no score of theirs exceeded 80; and only twice was 77 not matched or bettered.

Twelve years later, by which time Arnold Palmer had begun irrevocably to inaugurate the modern era of golf, Palmer successfully defended the championship. His record aggregate of 276 beat Kel Nagle by six strokes and Brian Huggett and Phil Rodgers, who were joint third, by another seven. Palmer won so comprehensively because, as he later declared, he declined 'to let myself get locked into a life and death struggle with the course,' now more than 7,000 yards long, but baked hard by a prolonged drought.

Jack Nicklaus, who had beaten Palmer in a play-off for the US Open a month before, his first victory as a professional, finished fifth to last, twenty-nine strokes behind. Nicklaus's subsequent contributions to the rehabilitation of the championship to world ranking need no rehearsing here. Palmer's triumph confirmed the old saying: 'Beware the unhealthy golfer.' He suffered variously from hip twinges, pains in the legs and arms, and a stomach upset. He also remarked, prophetically, of Nicklaus, 'Now that the big guy's out of the cage, everybody better run for cover.'

As significant in its way, this was the last of the old-style Opens. The pioneering example set later that year by the now-defunct Senior Service tournament at Dalmahoy, near Edinburgh, had impressed both the R & A and the golfing public. A grandstand was built by the eighteenth green, there was a tented village offering alternative attractions to the golf, and, against tradition, the first prize of £2,000 was £500 more than Palmer's reward had been. The Championship Committee were made aware of the need for improvements, specifically that raising the prize money might well be desirable, but it could only be increased if more spectators attended, and they would only be attracted if facilities were improved. For the players, exemptions from pre-qualifying were introduced the following year.

Thus when the Open returned to Troon eleven years later, improvements 'on the ground' had long since been implemented. Alerted by the undisciplined behaviour of some spectators at the climax of Palmer's victory, the R & A had 20,000 yards of fencing erected; the first three fairways were moved towards the beach; the sixth and twelfth greens were relocated, and five new tees were built. The championship itself proved, for Tom Weiskopf, a triumph of evolving mastery over initial misgivings. After a week of practice, Weiskopf still appeared confused as to how he should tackle the links, with their crumpled fairways and exposed greens. 'What do I do?' he asked. 'Go right out and kill it,' came the reply.

Crude as that advice sounded, it proved correct, for incessant rain slowed the course, 7,064 yards long, conditions which were ideally suited to Weiskopf's elegant power and the high trajectory of his shots.

Troon became a sort of home away from home, where Weiskopf had, as it happened, just won four times in his last seven outings. In effect, Weiskopf was asked to play the game he had brought to Scotland and with it he won convincingly, becoming the first player since Cotton in 1934 to lead from the start to finish and with a record-equalling aggregate of 276, beating Johnny Miller by three strokes. The keys which unlocked the door for Weiskopf were the length and accuracy of his driving and the fact that he never once took three putts.

Victory in a championship, Bernard Darwin once observed, whets the appetites of some players for more, whereas there are those for whom one turns out to be enough. Weiskopf fell into the latter group; Tom Watson, his successor in 1982, was very definitely a fully paid-up member of the other club. Having the previous month won the US Open in a most dramatic way, with the chip shot he holed at Pebble Beach's seventeenth, the seventy-first hole, to defeat Nicklaus, Watson was justifiably confident. He predicted a winning total of six under par (only two strokes too few, as it turned out) and asserted, 'I've developed the touch needed for a links course and I'm reading the greens well.' It was not plain sailing, though.

Indeed, victory for Watson, to give him his seventh major title in eight seasons and place him alongside Jones, Sarazen, Hogan and Trevino as the only players to win the British and US Opens in the same summer, looked particularly unlikely at two stages of the championship – at halfway and again in the very last hour of play. After thirty-six holes Watson, on 140, found himself seven strokes adrift of a fellow American, Bobby Clampett, aged twenty-two and competing in the Open for the first time. Needing only fifty-one putts, twenty-one of them singles, Clampett had scores of 67, 66 and led by five strokes, the widest margin after two rounds since Gary Player in 1974, and his total of 133 was only one higher than Cotton's record for the first thirty-six holes of the event.

Nick Price, who would be so closely and sadly involved in the outcome, was on 138, his two 69s giving him the distinction of having broken 70 four times in five successive Open rounds, and this in spite of having missed the cut in three of his previous seven tournaments. Clampett increased his lead to seven strokes after five holes of the third round when the wheels flew comprehensively off the juggernaut. He took eight at the sixth, at 577 yards the longest hole on a British championship course and which must have seemed endless to him after he had been in three bunkers. Clampett's final two rounds of 78, 77 gave him an aggregate twenty-two strokes higher than his first two, a fall from grace Price was to share in more anguished circumstances still.

After three successive birdies Price led by three strokes with only six holes to play. But he dropped four strokes over the next five holes for a 73 to finish runner-up (as he was to do again in 1988 to Severiano Ballesteros) with Peter Oosterhuis. Watson, who after returning what had seemed to be a fruitless 70, had to wait forty minutes to learn his fate. In becoming the third American in succession to win at what by now was Royal Troon – regalized four years earlier in the club's centenary year – Watson gained the fourth of his five Open Championships. With clinical conciseness Weiskopf summed up, 'When you are at the top as often as Tom Watson is, someone is bound to hand you one eventually.'

ARNOLD PALMER AND THE OPEN

BY MICHAEL McDONNELL

Future golf historians may conclude that two of the great milestones in twentieth century development were the mass exodus of a generation of young Scotsmen who took the basic game across the Atlantic in the early years and then the momentous return of one exceptional man who delivered it back to British shores polished and transformed.

The truth of it all is that Arnold Palmer will always hold more importance than the sum total of his major titles. His influence and stature extended far beyond arithmetical and statistical claims. Indeed the record books, which show a championship career spanning no more than seven successful years, tell precious little of the true story.

Moreover, Arnie holds the unforgotten and undimished esteem of those of us who beheld the breathtaking wonders he had performed on the game by establishing, unwittingly perhaps, a brand new philosophy in which the old virtues of caution and care were abandoned and replaced by a two-fisted aggression that was prepared to give as good as it got.

In a sense, the career of Arnold Palmer is clear testimony that Walter Hagen got it slightly wrong when he said golf was a game of 'How many?' and not 'How'. Not the way Arnie played it. It was the head-on Palmer style that gave this hitherto dry and crusty game a rip-roaring excitement never before seen on the restrained fairways of the world.

It was of course the way we all wanted to play – this towering force that overwhelmed the puny little golf ball, despatched it huge distances and contemptuously dismissed even the most savage terrain, tempest or gale that dared to get in the way.

For that alone Arnie deserves his place in sporting history as well as the undying gratitude of the thousands of tournament professionals who followed him because the indisputable fact is he alone turned golf into a spectator sport, as packed with knife-edged drama as any football or baseball game.

There were no compromises. It was full throttle all the way to glory, and if the gods were with him then he prevailed. Yet the inherent weakness of such blind courage is that sometimes it meets a nasty accident of its own making, although it has to be said that whether he was winning or losing Arnie held centre stage, the star of the show; the man they would rather watch take 80 than witness somebody else break 70.

Indeed it seemed for him that golf had to be a test of strength, both physical and spiritual against the course, his rivals, the elements and the pressure of the moment. His 1960 Masters win was typical of what was to become known as the Palmer Charge. That day, the press were already interviewing somebody else fairly certain he was the winner when Arnie birdied the last two holes to snatch the title by a stroke.

Much the same happened with his US Open triumph at Cherry Hills later that year when Mike Souchak looked as though he was progressing sensibly towards the title when Arnie sprang into devastating action with a last–round 65 to take that title too (and managing to stay clear of a promising young amateur called Jack Nicklaus from the Scioto Country Club who finished two strokes behind).

Suddenly the measured world of golf writing had to summon the more explosive adjectives to describe this man's exploits so that, in a sense, Arnie created a whole new vocabulary for the game, because even in his moments of disaster he could snatch defeat from the jaws of victory with a panache and vulnerability that made a devoted public warm to him even more.

In 1961, he needed a gentle seven-iron from the

middle of Augusta's last fairway to find the green and earn a par-four that would make him Masters champion. Instead he traced a suicidal route around the green from bunker to bunker for a double bogey six to allow an astonished Gary Player, watching this ritual from the clubhouse, to become champion.

In truth his failures really were as dramatic as his triumphs, and none more so than his 1966 US Open defeat which, because of its high drama, is wrongly held to be not only his last real chance of winning a major title but also the effective end of his championship career. In fact he finished runner-up again a year later and even nine years afterwards was still finishing among the top ten.

But that day Arnie had been seven strokes clear of Billy Casper, with nine holes to play at the Olympic Club in San Francisco, but by the time they stepped from the last green they were tied for a play-off. It was an astonishing turn of events and even the next day there was to be no respite because once again Casper made up ground to overtake Arnie to become champion.

When he stepped ashore to play in the 1960 Open at St Andrews, we had not seen his like before and there was already a sense of history about the occasion because he had the chance to emulate the great achievement of Ben Hogan who in 1953 captured the Masters, the US Open and the Open Championship in one season.

Now Arnie was on the same threshold. His last-gasp win over Venturi in the Masters, his breathless triumph over Souchak and others at Cherry Hills, left him needing only the Open for this particular hat-trick. He came agonizingly close but it was not to be, and there were those that week in St Andrews who felt he had shown uncharacteristic caution in earlier rounds and paid the price by losing the title by a single stroke to Kel Nagle.

But it was the promise he made in defeat that was to transform not only the Open Championship but golf itself throughout Europe, although he could not have realized it at the time. He said quite simply, 'I will keep coming back until I have won the Open.'

He did more than that, because long after his name had been engraved on the silver claret jug,

Arnie had become such an essential feature of the championship that, whisper it, rules were introduced to ensure that he and other past champions would always be welcomed back.

The cause-and-effect process of Arnie's influence can be told fairly simply. He was the best of his day and, as such, the man who set the standards. Thus those who wished to stand comparison had to follow his example.

Fairly soon, but not immediately, the Americans were back in force at the Open, though it has to be said that some high-quality performers, Cary Middlecoff and Byron Nelson among them, made occasional forays throughout the fifties in what has become known as the Open's fallow period after Hogan declined to come back to defend.

The unkind implication of course is that without the American challenge the Open Championship itself was somehow easier to win during this period, and that the monopoly by Bobby Locke and Peter Thomson bears testimony to this fact. It is a view which does little justice to the talents of those two men.

Not only was Locke so successful in the United States that he could only be stopped by the rule book, but Thomson himself at the height of the American invasion in 1965 at Royal Birkdale, took on them all – Arnie, Jack Nicklaus, Tony Lema – to win his fifth title.

Skill apart, what Arnie did was to broaden the public appeal of the sport on both sides of the Atlantic with his dare-devil style of play. He humanized the game, gave it flesh and blood and yet the fact that he was so immensely successful in that task should not be allowed to detract from the remarkable performances of those who had gone before him.

That said, he still managed to bring his own touch of drama to each of his successive victories in the Open. At Royal Birkdale they even erected a monument to him and his magnificent shot from a bush in the last round which he hammered with such force that, they say, the ground shook.

A little plaque in the embankment to right of the present sixteenth fairway (in those days it was the fifteenth) marks the spot where, in that 1961

Open, one solitary stroke defined the nature of this man, his strength, his weakness, courage and sheer determination that nothing, not even a bush, would stand between him and victory. His own waywardness had put him in crisis, but it had been balanced with such redemptive force that it did not seem to matter.

Then too there was the man's patent honesty. A year later at Troon (as it was then) he called a penalty on himself after his club grazed the sand on the backswing. Nobody else saw it. But Arnie knew. And that was all that mattered. He still became champion again.

And yet he was not merely the stuff of champions. He was an archetypal hero in the great American tradition. He was, as fathers used to say, exactly what they wanted their sons to become. Not as a golfer. But as a man.

Of course his pedigree was faultless and pure Hollywood. The dutiful and prudent son of a club professional; never allowed to swim in the pool at the club, but one day so rich that he would buy the entire establishment (and still not swim in the pool). He was the first of multi-millionaires and such was his charisma that he could have run for political office, yet such too was his love of golf that he wanted nothing else but to play the game. Nor does he even to this day.

Moreover, it is a measure of his enduring integrity to a public, many of whom never played the game, that his name and reputation could be entrusted to market anything from dry-cleaning stores to sunglasses. If Arnie approved, then it had to be good.

It is possible to argue that he came along at precisely the right historical and economic moment as the western world boomed, standards of living rose and people began to set their sights towards the good life that encompassed not only more leisure time but also activities that hitherto had not seemed appropriate for the likes of them.

Perhaps. But the fact remains that he symbolized the game of golf to his generation and those who followed and he showed that it not only could be thrilling as well as immensely rewarding, but that there were no social barriers to the game either.

And yet while due tribute must be paid to the way Arnie restored the Open Championship, one part of the process has not been highlighted as fully as it deserves because it was not simply the revival of American interest that relaunched the Open as the major championship of the world.

Rather, it was the growing European response it provoked, starting with Tony Jacklin. From these beginnings did the game spread through Europe and lead to the establishment of a professional circuit whose very best performers – Sandy Lyle, Nick Faldo, Seve Ballesteros, Bernhard Langer and Ian Woosnam – stood comparison with their counterparts in the United States (as two Ryder Cup triumphs were to prove).

Here too, it is possible to detect the hand of Arnie because Tony Jacklin unashamedly used him as a role model (even to the trouser-tugging and the frown) to become champion on both sides of the Atlantic, as well as making himself a fortune in the process.

It meant that we could take our golf seriously again. And when Jacklin became the man to emulate, then Sandy, Seve, Nick and Bernhard followed him first on the American tour, then into the major championships and eventually into firmly entrenched positions at the top of the Sony World Ranking.

This then is the success story that began almost thirty years ago when Arnie came to play. But it was not the reason the fans turned out to pay homage to the old campaigner as he returned to Royal Troon for certainly his last competitive appearance in an Open there. Not a bit of it.

The old charismatic spark is still there. Nobody really cared about his scores at Royal Troon this time. For his loyal army of fans, he was engaged in a tumultuous lap of honour and he was cheered to every tee and down every fairway.

There were many reasons for such warmth; admiration for what he had achieved personally; gratitude for what he had given the game, particularly in Europe. But most of all, there was a shared joy that this man as he approached sixty still relished the fight, the challenge and the excitement of being involved. Win or lose. That gave us all the greatest hope. And that is why we cheered.

BEFORE THE
FIRST SHOT IS STRUCK

BY MARK WILSON

Officially, the 118th Open Championship began at 7.15 a.m. on Thursday 20 July, when the starter, Ivor Robson, called Charlie Bolling to the first tee of the Royal Troon Golf Club, and the American responded with a perfect drive. In reality, however, much had already been happening for three hours, since 4.05 a.m. to be precise. It was then that an alarm clock shattered the silence and darkness of room 318 in the Marine Highland Hotel, tight beside the eighteenth hole, and the four-star home for some of the world's greatest golfers throughout the championship. Arnold Palmer, Jack Nicklaus, Lee Trevino, Greg Norman and Tom Watson were a few of the celebrated guests.

In room 318, the person who came awake was Alan Turner, a retired cloth manufacturer from Leeds with a tireless enthusiasm for golf administration after reaching international standard as an amateur. It was time for Turner to set up the course and supervise the cutting of the holes for the Championship Committee. It was an unheralded, onerous responsibility he had shouldered for five years. Others saw it as a thankless task. Get it right and nothing was said; get so much as one flagstick in a position that makes its fairness vulnerable to changes in the weather, however unexpected, and there could be cruel recriminations. Turner, who looks, feels and works like a man ten years younger than his age, enjoys the challenge.

It was still dark when Turner stood on the first tee at 4.30 a.m., and joined James Armour, the Royal Troon Greens Convenor. Turner was armed with a weather forecast. Rightly, it warned of an extremely unusual south-east wind, very different to the conditions in which the practice rounds had been played. It also said rain wouldn't be a first-day factor. It was drizzling, and becoming increasingly uncomfortable

as he read it. Turner shrugged his broad shoulders, laughed and went to work by personally resetting the tee boxes to a pristine area. Walking the first fairway as night reluctantly surrendered to dawn, he remembered 1952, when Old Troon, as it was before becoming Royal, had been the stage for his international baptism for England. His opponent that day, Ireland's John Glover, is now secretary to the Royal and Ancient's Rules Committee.

Norman Fergusson, the Royal Troon greenkeeper, an incredibly loyal, dedicated and knowledgeable general in that great army of Scots whose expertise is a vital part of the backbone of golf, was waiting on the first green. 'What about this weather?' chided Turner. 'I've been on my knees asking for rain these past three months,' answered Fergusson. 'Now it comes when we don't want it.'

There is nothing haphazard about determining the pin placements at the Open Championship. Turner had spent two days studying the greens and selecting the most likely positions for the cutting of the holes on each of the four rounds. But flexibility to meet the demands of uncooperative weather is an essential part of the process. It was used at the first green where Turner tossed down a tee peg to mark the spot shown on his preconceived plan. After a 360–degree walk, and a look at the heavy clouds above, he changed his mind. The possibility of more rain later in the day made a move to higher ground a wise precaution.

The tee peg was dropped again; Armour nodded his approval, so did Fergusson, and with hands made enormously strong by forty-six years of greenkeeping service, Turner plunged his hole cutter into the manicured green. Within seconds, the job was done, including a neat trimming of the rim with a pair of specially made scissors almost semi-circular in shape.

Then Fergusson's son, Alan, stepped forward with brush and paint to whiten the inside top inch of the hole. 'It's an aid for the TV cameras,' he explained. 'I did the same job at the last Open here, in 1982, and it rained so much then that I had trouble making the paint stick. I remember one of the commentators saying it was difficult to see some of the holes, and that hurt.'

The caravan moved on to the second hole, Fergusson travelling in his modern work-horse, a battered Land Rover that copes with every challenge at the sacrifice of comfort. As he bounced up and down in the driver's seat, he spoke of his life since he had been born sixty-two years before in the house beside the sixteenth fairway. It was the home of his father from whom he inherited the role of greenkeeper. 'It's deep in the blood,' he said in a voice that rang with pride. 'My grandfather was the greenkeeper just down the road at Prestwick St Nicholas.' Just then a particularly severe hump caused the Land Rover to become airborne. 'They had really hard lives,' Fergusson declared in a matter-of-fact voice. 'I remember my father having to get about the course on a bicycle no matter how bad the weather.'

A diversion added interest to the task at the third hole. All night, each of the eighteen greens had been patrolled by a security guard. On approaching, armed with the cutter that might have passed for a rocket launcher in the lingering gloom, we were challenged. It took a radio call to base – 'I have five gentlemen here who say they are officials wanting to cut a hole in the green' – to satisfy the security guard that we were on a mission of peace. After a long, wet night of vigil, he was doing his job, and doing it well.

By now, Turner, associated all his golfing life with Moortown, a former Yorkshire Amateur champion, and a member of the Championship Committee for many years, including being the deputy chairman in 1985, was warming, figuratively if not literally in the continuing drizzle, to his task. 'The uppermost thought in my mind is fairness,' he confided. 'I do not think about setting the course up to defy low scoring. It doesn't worry me if they shoot 63s, so long as it is a fair test of ability and in keeping with the traditions of the championship. It has to look right. I don't like

seeing a pin position stuck in some odd corner just to make life difficult. I have played the game a bit, and I know what is wanted.'

The eighth hole, the Postage Stamp, at 126 yards the shortest in championship golf, riddled with history, caused the greatest change in Turner's plan. He had the pin down for bottom left of the green; the now steady rain convinced him that top right would be the wisest precaution against possible flooding. Hardly had the decision been taken and the hole cut and painted than Graeme Simmers, chairman of the Championship Committee, arrived on the scene. He had a new, up-to-the-minute weather forecast. 'The rain won't worry us,' he announced. 'It will stop soon.' Well-drenched, Turner, Fergusson and Armour shared a rueful smile.

On the tenth green Fergusson revealed a sense of humour as he told a strange story against himself. Several years ago a Scottish Amateur championship was suspended overnight because of flooded greens. Next morning, guided by a forecast that warned of more torrential rain to come, he cut a new hole on higher ground at the tenth. Later he was trying to enjoy a quick breakfast when the news arrived about one very unhappy player. Unknown to anyone, the player had marked his ball the night before rather than putt out when play was suspended. On returning to the tenth green to face what had been a putt of two feet, he found he was forty feet from the new position.

The sight of his home from the sixteenth fairway had Fergusson in a wistful mood. 'Sixty-two years in the same house, every day I've lived, left to raise my family in peace and quiet, gives me a lot to think about. I know the day will come when I must retire and leave to start another kind of life. I try not to think about it too much.' When he does move on, there won't be any more young Fergussons to continue the family tradition of greenkeeping. Alan, his son, has chosen to become an insurance broker. 'The boy has a good job in a good profession, and I wouldn't argue with him,' says an understanding father.

Happily, Fergusson still has a gifted successor to hand on to golf. He has trained a young mem-

ber of his staff so well that the lad has won the National Greenkeeper Apprentice of the Year award. Fergusson watches him at work, and beams with a special sense of pride. 'It's a hard career at times,' he concedes. 'But it's a good life, too, and getting better.' No more does he have to spend sleepless nights watering greens with a hose-pipe as at the 1950 Open Championship.

Suddenly, the hole-cutting caravan was invaded by three caddies whose job it was to follow behind with a surveyor's wheel and make precise measurements of the pin placements so that detailed maps could be made as an aid for all competitors that day.

It was now 6.30 a.m., the first player was off in forty-five minutes, and there was no time to waste. By 6.50 a.m. the task was completed. Michael Bonallack, secretary of the Royal and Ancient, his deputy George Wilson, and Graeme Simmers express

their appreciation as a final cut is given to the eighteenth green by Fergusson's brother Billy, another member of the Royal Troon greenkeeping staff.

Turner, duty done until the next morning, headed back to room 318 and his bed at the Marine Highland Hotel. On the first tee, Ivor Robson called for Charlie Bolling, and the gallery applauded the start of the 118th Open Championship, not knowing all that had been happening for the past three hours to get the championship under way.

A jubilant Wayne Stephens, with a 66, led the first day.

FORTY-ONE
PLAYERS ARE UNDER PAR

BY MICHAEL WILLIAMS

There is before each Open Championship a war of words. Last year at Royal Lytham, Tony Jacklin, Europe's Ryder Cup captain, set the cat amongst the pigeons when he said that he could not see other than a European winning and he was right, for Severiano Ballesteros became the champion. This year at Royal Troon it was the turn of the bookmakers. They quoted odds of five-to-two against a first American victory since 1983.

If this was not exactly a red flag to a bull, it certainly prompted a positive response from Tom Kite, who was still getting over the acute disappointment of losing the United States Open at Oak Hill after leading by three strokes with fourteen holes to play.

'There is understandably tremendous pride in Europe right now,' said Kite, 'because Seve, Nick (Faldo), Ian (Woosnam) and Sandy (Lyle) are as good as any players in the world. But don't downgrade the Americans. We are not dogs, and can play a little bit too. For somebody in the Press or some bookie to say the Americans can't play is not very accurate and not very smart either. I think that to a certain extent there may have been a little over-reaction on the part of the fans and maybe the media over here, as to what has happened in the last few years, particularly in the Ryder Cup. In fact, they have all been very close matches.'

Tom Watson, back on the course where he had won the fourth of his five Opens in 1982, was less incensed. 'The way the championship has gone in the last five years, that is reasonable judgement on the part of the bookies,' he thought, deciding nevertheless that he 'would have a slice of it' and at the same time something on himself since at forty-to-one, it was too good an opportunity to pass by.

Watson said that he could remember vividly his last round here in 1982. 'I played very well and

strong,' he recalled, 'and it brings back a strong winning feeling. If I can translate that into the rest of my game, which is right on the verge of breaking through, then something might happen very good for Tom Watson here at the British Open.'

Curtis Strange, who had won the American Open a month earlier, reported himself more 'fired up' than he could remember for an Open, but what was somewhat unexpected after so many rotten years for weather was a sun-kissed Royal Troon links, the higher points of the fairways burned brown and the rough much lighter than usual, particularly on the outward half. It was, as Strange observed, very different from recent conditions in America, where it had rained almost incessantly with the result that 'where we hit the ball it had stuck, both on the fairways and on the greens.' Nevertheless, Strange was not going to change his style of play, only his mental attitude, 'because you have to get used to the bounces, sometimes good and sometimes bad.'

Greg Norman, who was not exactly enthusiastic about the general state of his game, nevertheless welcomed the return to a hard and fast links and, like most of the other leading contenders, hoped for a wind to sort out the men from the boys. Ballesteros was optimistic, even going so far as to say that his game was better now than it had been going into the Open twelve months earlier; while Faldo, who wore the mantle of favourite, indicated that he had tightened the last of the nuts and bolts and needed only to slip into gear.

Of one thing everyone was convinced, and that was that the weather would not last. They were wrong. It did. Apart from the Friday morning, when it was overcast with the odd spatter of rain, this was to become a championship dominated by sunshine with none of the swift changes of weather often associated with the turning of the tide out on the shore. The wind, while from time to time switching direction, never became more than a gentle summer breeze and Royal Troon could seldom have played more gently.

There was an astounding total of forty-one players under par and another nineteen players were level par on the first day.

This pattern of low scoring was evident right from the start when, beginning with Lee Trevino, who at forty-nine is on the threshold of senior status and led either on his own or jointly through the first two rounds of the Masters, no less than seven players recorded scores of 68. The others comprised two more Americans in Fred Couples and Paul Azinger, two Spaniards in Jose-Maria Olazabal and Miguel Martin, an Argentinian in Eduardo Romero, and an Australian, Wayne Grady.

Hot on their heels came another eight players, all with 69. There was a European quartet in Philip Walton, of Ireland, Brian Marchbank, Derrick Cooper and Mark James, two Americans, Watson and Steve Pate, Australia's Norman and one South African, Gavin Levenson. With therefore fifteen players within a stroke of one another, it was as confusing a picture as there had ever been, the Press tent scratching its combined head as it tried to work out the best 'story' until, as afternoon gave way to evening, another name, Stephens, appeared on the leaderboard at four under par.

Record books were hastily unearthed and it transpired that Stephens' name was Wayne, that he was twenty-eight years old, born in Jersey, had been to the qualifying school seven times and was currently 121st in the European money list with earnings of £10,400. And that was about it. Under such circumstances it was widely assumed that Stephens, who had gone out in 32, would surely collapse at any minute, particularly since the inward half at Royal Troon is much harder than the first nine holes.

Instead Stephens did indeed hold on; pars through the next five holes and then suddenly he went to the top of the board on his own with a five-iron second to the fifteenth green and a putt for a birdie from twelve feet. Still there were those that doubted him, but far from taking fright, Stephens, with his shock of fair hair and a cigarette or two to steady his nerves, then holed from eighteen feet for a two at the seventeenth and with a 66 led the field by two strokes.

Not surprisingly, Stephens was almost in a state of shock as he confronted the world's Press. 'It's a dream come true,' he said, 'a marvellous feeling I have at the moment, though I don't think it has sunk in yet.' Here he was, a struggling professional leading the best professionals in the world in the oldest championship of them all. And, what is more, in his first Open.

As a native of Jersey, Stephens shares the same birthplace as Harry Vardon, who won the Open six times at the turn of the century, but he confirmed that golf has been a real struggle. He first got his player's card in 1984, lost it immediately and had to turn to regional golf as an assistant club professional at in turn Royal Jersey, Royal Mid-Surrey and Coombe Wood. In 1987 he regained his card, lost it again and then got it back in the autumn of 1988.

At one point Stephens had even considered giving the game up, but his career took a turn for the better when he came under the influence of Terry Hanson, the professional at Cardiff. 'We worked out a swing change about six weeks ago,' said Stephens. 'I was not sure whether it was right or not, but Terry insisted it was and I have played the most solid golf of my life since. We moved the ball position forward and I have got a better release.'

'It was nerve-racking out there to say the least. Normally I get through six or seven cigarettes a round; today it was fifteen. I went out with the attitude of just enjoying it and kept going for the middle of the green.'

At first Stephens played almost in isolation, his gallery being made up of his father, Graham, and Jack Steele, a former captain of Irvine Bogside (where Stephens qualified) who was putting him up for the week because he had no accommodation. But by the time Stephens had made a third consecutive birdie at the fifth with a long putt, one or two more began to follow him, rewarded as he then made a fourth birdie at the seventh, this time with a drive and eight iron to four feet.

'I was just trying to wear blinkers and not think about it,' said Stephens, 'but when I made three at fifteen the roar was deafening and at seventeen it was just incredible. You have to harden yourself to the pressures but I was getting more confident the longer the round went.' Indeed the only time he was in any sort of trouble was at the last where he was bunkered off the tee. However, he played a fine wedge to four feet, holed the putt for his par and therefore kept a clean sheet in that his round did not include a single bogey.

It was quite like old times to see Trevino setting the pace earlier with his 68, though ironically a bigger gallery was with the match ahead, watching Strange, who played with great competence for a 70 that could hardly have been any more than that. It was not less because he was constantly thirty to forty feet away on the greens, too far to have any real expectation of birdies.

Trevino, on the other hand, had a run of three birdies in a row from the fourth only to drop shots at the seventh and eighth. Then, with the wind blowing over his right shoulder and countering therefore the fade he naturally gets on the ball, he played the inward half in 33 with birdies at the fourteenth, fifteenth and eighteenth, single putting indeed all of the last five greens.

His three at the last was a real beauty, a four iron out of the light rough to eighteen feet, pin high left and then a putt that never looked anywhere but in the hole. 'It's a long time since I felt so good,' he said afterwards. 'This is the type of course I can play. Experience brings you patience and that is what the Open is all about.'

Faldo launched himself typically and uneventfully with a 71 that included seventeen pars and one birdie, at the eleventh. It was another of his frustrating rounds with little reward on the greens and what chance there was of birdies at the two long holes going out, the fourth and sixth, spoiled by drives left and then right into thick rough. When in trouble at the last two holes, Faldo each time played exquisite bunker shots to keep his head above water.

Consequently he was eclipsed by Couples, who said he benefited from playing with Faldo in that he learned something of course management. Nevertheless Couples was honest enough to admit that 68 was about the best he could have done. The possessor of one of the longer swings in professional golf, Couples is also one of the longer hitters and he made birdies at all the par fives, though reaching only the eleventh in two shots. He also made a two at the fifth, scrambled two other pars but three-putted the eighth.

Grady, who was subsequently to play one of the lead roles in the destiny of the championship, had a new-found confidence after recently winning the Westchester tournament in America, his first victory in the States. He too got away to a good start with a 68 though for once his driving, normally his strongest suit, was this time his weakest. 'I just kept popping them in the air,' he said.

Prior to his victory at Westchester, Grady had missed eight cuts in eleven tournaments, but with that landmark behind him he declared that he had a better chance of winning this week than ever before. Four of his five birdies were made on the outward half and he was looking at a 67 until he missed the green at the seventeenth.

No one had better reason to thank his lucky stars than Martin, one of the less celebrated Spaniards, but one who has nevertheless shown initiative by going to America and obtaining his player's card. His good fortune this week was that he got into the Open only as the first alternate, missing out in a play-off at Barassie but getting the call when the American, Jay Haas, withdrew.

He certainly took his chance, making four consecutive birdies from the eighth, two others at the earlier par fives but dropping shots both at the fifth, where he was bunkered, and at the long sixteenth, where he took three putts.

Azinger, runner-up to Faldo at Muirfield in 1987, began with a bogey-five and made his 68 largely with a burst of birdies over the closing holes, at the fourteenth, sixteenth and eighteenth, where his five-iron approach stopped almost on the very lip of the hole. Azinger had gone out prepared to play a patient round, avoiding trouble and just getting himself into position. Four under par was as welcome to him as it also exceeded expectation.

Lee Trevino (opposite page) revived old memories;
(clockwise from top left): Wayne Grady (68) was fresh off a
victory in America, Jose-Maria Olazabal (68) continued his
good form in major championships, Peter Jacobsen (71)
was among the American challengers, and Miguel Martin
(68) added to the Spanish threat.

U S Open champion Curtis Strange (top) returned a solid 70, which was his best of the week, and defending Open champion Seve Ballesteros (bottom) had three putts to lip out, a signal that this would not be his time to win.

Romero, recognized as a long hitter, made the most of the par fives with an eagle-three at the fourth and birdie-fours at the other three. He played well in the Open last year, too, finishing thirteenth. His only dropped stroke came at the thirteenth, which with the fifteenth presents one of the major obstacles to the Royal Troon finish. Conversely Olazabal made threes at both, albeit with substantial putts, but that was the feature of his 68 and the happy result of his moving the ball closer to him at the address, a tip suggested by Anders Forsbrand.

Ballesteros began disappointingly but not disastrously with a 72. He had been looking to be two or three under par going out, was instead level and always therefore had his back to the wall. He found it difficult to judge distances and the bounce of the ball, and when he might have made birdies at the twelfth, thirteenth and fifteenth, the ball each time lipped out.

One of the more eventful rounds was Watson's 69. Having negotiated the outward half in 33, he seemed to be sailing serenely along but then made three bogeys, two of them even then with single putts. That he got home in nothing worse than 36 was due to an eagle-three at the eleventh, where he chipped in (if his ball had not hit the stick, it would have gone some thirty feet past) and then a three at the last.

Norman's 69 was also in the long run a significant contribution. He had an inkling that he might play well because he felt nervous walking to the first tee and when keyed up like that he cannot wait to get started. In fact a dropped shot at the second was not a good beginning, but he was aggressive with his putts, often having to hole the one back from three or four feet. Soon he had the red figures up against his name and altogether he did very little wrong.

The day was nevertheless not without its disasters, and none more so than that which overcame Sandy Lyle, who had been going through such a lean patch but, much to the delight of the Scottish crowd, seemed about to jump right into the thick of things with a 70. Alas, his seven-iron second shot to the eighteenth caught a hard spot and bounced through the green and on to the shale path underneath the

clubhouse windows and therefore out of bounds. Lyle, hitting his fourth into a television buggy, finished with a seven for 73, one less than Ian Woosnam, whose 74 was all about an inward half of 40.

Nor was Lyle alone in recording a seven. So did Kite, who had gone out in 31 with three birdies and an eagle. He then came a cropper at the fifteenth where he went out of bounds. It turned a possible 67 into a 70, but at least it was done early enough for Kite this time to repair the damage.

On a day of predictably low scoring, it was easy not to take much notice of anyone who failed to score under 70. It was therefore excusable to see no significance in a 71 from Mark Calcavecchia. But his was a profile that was to remain low for some time yet.

Both on 69, Derrick Cooper (top) credited his score to being relaxed and Philip Walton (bottom) said he got a lucky break and a free drop at No. 11. Paul Azinger (following page) had a late burst of birdies for his 68.

For some, the first round of the Open was like a day at the beach, and others only watched the golf from afar.

FIRST ROUND RESULTS

HOLE	1	2	3	4	5	6	7	8	9	10	11	12	13	14	15	16	17	18	
PAR	4	4	4	5	3	5	4	3	4	4	5	4	4	3	4	5	3	4	TOTAL
Wayne Stephens	4	4	3	4	2	5	3	3	4	4	5	4	4	3	3	5	2	4	66
Lee Trevino	4	4	4	4	2	4	5	4	4	4	5	4	4	2	3	5	3	3	68
Fred Couples	4	4	4	4	2	4	4	4	4	4	4	4	4	3	4	4	3	4	68
Eduardo Romero	4	4	4	3	3	4	4	3	4	4	4	5	3	4	4	4	3	4	68
Paul Azinger	5	4	4	4	3	5	3	3	4	3	5	4	5	2	4	4	3	3	68
Miguel Martin	4	4	4	4	4	4	4	2	3	3	4	4	4	3	4	6	3	4	68
Wayne Grady	4	4	4	4	3	4	3	2	4	4	4	4	4	3	4	5	4	4	68
Jose-Maria Olazabal	4	3	4	4	3	6	3	3	4	5	5	4	3	3	3	4	3	4	68
Philip Walton	4	4	3	4	3	5	4	3	5	4	4	4	3	3	3	5	3	5	69
Brian Marchbank	3	5	4	5	3	5	4	2	5	3	4	3	5	3	4	4	3	4	69
Derrick Cooper	4	4	4	4	2	5	5	3	4	4	5	3	4	3	3	4	4	4	69
Greg Norman	4	5	4	4	3	4	4	3	3	4	4	4	3	4	5	5	3	4	69
Steve Pate	4	4	4	3	2	5	4	3	4	4	4	4	4	3	5	5	3	4	69
Mark James	3	4	3	3	3	5	4	4	5	4	4	4	5	2	4	5	3	4	69
Tom Watson	4	4	3	4	3	4	4	3	4	5	3	5	4	3	5	5	3	3	69
Gavin Levenson	3	4	4	5	3	4	3	3	4	4	5	4	4	4	4	5	2	4	69

HOLE SUMMARY

HOLE	PAR	EAGLES	BIRDIES	PARS	BOGEYS	HIGHER	RANK	AVERAGE
1	4	0	13	113	29	1	11	4.12
2	4	0	11	110	34	1	9	4.16
3	4	0	20	108	25	3	13	4.08
4	5	7	50	80	19	0	17	4.71
5	3	0	17	99	38	2	5	3.16
6	5	4	39	82	26	5	15	4.93
7	4	0	22	96	32	6	10	4.14
8	3	0	28	98	25	5	13	3.06
9	4	0	14	101	36	5	6	4.21
OUT	36	11	214	887	264	28		36.57
10	4	0	10	91	51	4	2	4.31
11	5	2	71	65	14	4	18	4.67
12	4	0	14	103	35	4	8	4.19
13	4	0	15	94	46	1	6	4.21
14	3	0	19	107	29	1	12	3.08
15	4	0	21	87	39	9	4	4.25
16	5	1	38	96	21	0	16	4.88
17	3	0	8	96	50	2	1	3.29
18	4	0	10	102	38	6	3	4.27
IN	36	3	206	841	323	31		37.15
TOTAL	72	14	420	1728	587	59		73.72

			LOW SCORES		
Players Below Par	41				
Players At Par	19		Low First Nine	Gene Sauers	30
Players Above Par	96		Low Second Nine	Paul Azinger	33
				Brian Marchbank	33
				Lee Trevino	33
			Low Round	Wayne Stephens	66

Fred Couples was among the American contenders.

DAY
2
REVIVING MEMORIES
OF VICTORY

BY MICHAEL WILLIAMS

It was in 1914 that Harry Vardon won his sixth and last Open Championship at Prestwick, the spire of whose church can be seen from Royal Troon, the two courses indeed almost abutting one another, divided now only by Prestwick's international airport. Seventy-five years on, the record still stands, though four players have won five times: James Braid and J.H. Taylor, who were contemporaries of Vardon, Peter Thomson between 1954 and 1965 and Tom Watson between 1975 and 1983.

After Watson's victory at Royal Birkdale on the last of these five occasions, nothing seemed more certain than that he would equal Vardon's record. He was then after all only thirty-three and in his prime. But as the years have gone by, that dream has remained a dream, as his gifts seemed slowly to desert him until even he must have wondered whether the chance would ever come again. It was as if the gods could not quite decide whether Watson was fit to stand alongside so revered a golfing legend as Vardon.

This day however, Watson, now approaching his fortieth birthday, rose again from the ashes of a career that had seen him win only one tournament in five years. He conjured a 68 from some of Royal Troon's more unlikely places for a share of second place with another American, Payne Stewart, who returned a 65, both of them two strokes behind Wayne Grady, of Australia. Grady, after a 68 on Thursday, had followed with a 67.

So Watson stood exactly where he had stood seven years ago on the same Ayrshire links, second then to Bobby Clampett after thirty-six holes, though then the difference was six strokes, three times greater than it was now. Nevertheless Watson had come through, first as Clampett collapsed in a heap and then by courtesy of Nick Price, who had

frittered away a three-stroke lead over the last six holes.

As Watson had said before the 1989 championship began, Royal Troon 'revived strong memories' and there was much about his golf on this strange second day that was reminiscent of Watson in his prime, even he being moved to admit that this was a 'typical Tom Watson mixed grill' of escape and unlikely opportunity grabbed.

It was a strange day because the leader–board took shape under the grey skies and light rain of the morning and then remained virtually unaltered as the sun began to break through in conditions in the afternoon that no one could have claimed to have been even remotely difficult. By four o'clock the crowds, more than 33,000, which brought the total for the week to 95,000, were leaving in droves in the knowledge that the halfway picture was complete. Of the leading seventeen players at the end of the day, only four began their rounds after eleven o'clock.

After the high expectation that had centred on the big European battalions before the championship began, they were now more conspicuous by their absence. Ian Woosnam, improving by two strokes with a 72, made the cut with nothing to spare and so did Sandy Lyle, who repeated his 73. Severiano Ballesteros was similarly conspicuous after rounds of 72, 73 and only Nick Faldo was even faintly still in the hunt with another 71 but now seven strokes behind Grady.

Instead, the European challenge rested in the hands of David Feherty, an engaging and cheerful Ulsterman, who had a sparkling 67 and advanced to a three-way share of fourth place with Eduardo Romero, of Argentina, and Wayne Stephens. Stephens, the hero of the first day, did not blink under the glare of the spotlight and played very well for this time a level-par 72.

Two other Europeans, Derrick Cooper (70) and Mark James (70), also advanced their cause to stand four strokes off the lead together with Greg Norman (70) and five Americans in Steve Pate (70), Scott Simpson (66), Fred Couples (71), Mark Calcavecchia (68) and Mark McCumber (68).

With Paul Azinger (73), Tommy Armour (71), Lee Trevino (71), Raymond Floyd (68), Johnny Miller (69) and Michael Allen (67), who had won the Bell's Scottish Open the previous week, all tucked in with Miguel Martin, of Spain, and two more Australians in Ian Baker-Finch and Jeffrey Woodland, there were therefore fourteen Americans in the top twenty-six and a boot was beginning to be laced on a once-familiar foot.

Inevitably there were casualties as the cut fell on 146, two over par. Out went Nick Price, runner-up to Ballesteros at Royal Lytham a year ago, Jeff Sluman, the American PGA champion, Fuzzy Zoeller, Andy Bean, and other former champions in Tom Weiskopf, Gary Player, Tony Jacklin and Arnold Palmer.

If Palmer was – and indeed still is in many ways – one of the great heroes of the game, so too is Watson in the eyes of the British public, perhaps even more so than he is in America. His love of links golf, shining honesty, good manners and humility have been much admired and no one has treated those twin impostors, triumph and disaster, with greater equanimity.

Watson had an inkling that his game might be coming back when, with Byron Nelson, he stopped en route to Royal Troon to play in Ireland, at Ballybunion, Rosses Point and Royal County Down – all a new experience to Nelson – and perhaps it was there that Watson got his putting stroke back.

He holed from fifteen feet for a birdie at the second, saved par from the same distance at the fourth and sank a thirty-footer for a birdie at the fifth. Pars were also saved at the ninth and tenth and another break came at the eleventh, the Railway Hole, a not long but very treacherous par five. Watson hooked from the tee but had the good fortune to run through some whins on to a grass path trodden flat by spectators. From there he made a birdie when he could well have been unplayable.

But the biggest bonus, after a further more conventional birdie at the twelfth, came at the sixteenth, where he was in one of the right-hand bunkers beside the green with a three-wood second and then holed the next for an eagle-three. Certainly a shot was still to be dropped at the last, but even so a 68 left Watson in a good position to win. 'Now it is a question of doing it,' he said.

By then Grady was already in with his 67 for 135, having played what he described as 'smart golf', which was another way of saying that he had done nothing silly, letting things happen instead of trying to force them. He missed only two greens, the seventeenth and eighteenth, but each time got up and down from bunkers and therefore did not run up a single bogey. These small mistakes, neither of which cost him anything, were nevertheless not untypical of Grady, who admits to sometimes getting ahead of himself with thoughts of finishing, rather than just concentrating on the next shot.

'I'm driving well, hitting my irons and putting well,' he summarized. 'In fact I'm doing everything pretty well. So far I have not hit the ball in a spot where I have been in any trouble. I'm sure I will be a little jittery tomorrow when I tee off, but I hope it will make me concentrate harder. I'm a pretty determined person, although a slow developer but the urge has always been there.'

That development had an uncertain start for Grady, having turned professional at sixteen, got his amateur status back within a matter of months. Then he became a professional again in 1978 and came under the influence of Charlie Earp, Norman's coach, at Royal Queensland. Later he was to attack both the Asian and European circuits, where he won the German Open in 1984, though all the time he had his eye on America, which he saw as the pinnacle.

Stewart had knocked on the door of many a major championship without yet succeeding in having it opened. But now here he was again with a record 65 because the eighteenth hole had been lengthened by fifty yards, accommodating also a new bunker on the left. It was a landmark that carried little significance for him. 'Course records mean nothing unless you win the tournament,' he said, making a mistake common among Americans in that they seldom refer to this or even the US Open as a championship.

Dressed as usual in pastel-coloured plus twos, Stewart had been acutely disappointed with his 72 in the first round, and his wife had suggested that he got out of bed on the other side for he had been stony-faced all that previous day. 'Maybe that did it,' he speculated. At all events, he felt thoroughly comfortable with his game and particularly when the putter was in his hand, for he had the feeling that he could 'hole it from anywhere' as the light rain took some of the sting out of the putting surfaces.

This was Stewart's sixth successive Open after playing for the first time in 1981 and then missing a couple of years. He has become acclimatized to the changing character of a links, noting how today he had hit an eight-iron second to the thirteenth green whereas it had been a two iron in the first round.

'Seaside golf tests your patience and imagination,' he said, and there was a good illustration of it at the sixth hole, by which time he was already two under par after birdies at the second and fourth. Short of the green in two, he elected to take his putter from the fairway and holed it from sixty feet for an eagle-three.

With the wind behind him, Stewart was able to reach the eleventh with a seven-iron second for another birdie, sank a big putt for a birdie-two at the fourteenth and after throwing a shot away at the fifteenth, came back to finish four, three, three, a twenty-foot putt at the last after an eight-iron second setting the record.

The Irish were out in force after Feherty and very proud he did them, for his 67 that could also have been a 65. He dropped two shots in the last three holes, though it never wiped the cherry grin from his face as he acknowledged friends all along the way.

It was blistering stuff for a long time with an outward half of 31. Feherty had birdies at the first, fourth, fifth, sixth and eighth, adding two more at the eleventh and thirteenth, all of them with putts of between six and twelve feet. It was disappointing therefore that he took six at the sixteenth, risking a wooden-club second shot between the bunkers and instead dragging it left into thick rough.

From there Feherty could not control the ball, found a bunker, came out well but missed the putt that would have saved his par. Then at the last he mis-hit his drive shot and left and even went so far as to play a provisional. In fact the lie was a reasonable one but he could not remotely get home in two, nor save himself after that.

Romero began indifferently with fives at both the first and second, wryly blaming it on having to get up at 5 a.m. for one of the earliest starting times. But once he got the sleep out of his eyes, he came back with birdies at the sixth, eighth, eleventh and twelfth. 'My strength has been my driving and long irons,' he explained, reminiscent indeed of his boyhood hero, Roberto de Vicenzo, who in his time has given him advice on golfing matters.

After all the attention he had received on Thursday, Stephens could have been excused some reaction, especially too when his normal fifteen-minute drive to the course became an hour and twenty-five minutes because of heavy traffic. If it limited his time on the practice round, it made no difference. With birdie fours at the fourth and sixth – after a character-building five-foot putt to save par at the first – Stephens was off and running again.

Two unkind bounces then led to dropped strokes at the eighth and ninth but the spirit remained strong in a bit of a topsy-turvy inward half with one shot dropped at the thirteenth, two at the short fourteenth, where he chipped into a bunker, but three birdies elsewhere including a chip-in at the fifteenth.

In many ways the most spectacular round of the day was Simpson's 66 for it included nine birdies, five of them on the inward half and three in the last four holes – unusual for Royal Troon. However, there were three bogeys as well, which probably explained Simpson's analysis that 'I could have hit the ball better'. If it seemed at the time a significant move, so too in the long run was Calcavecchia's 68.

'I'm in good shape,' Calcavecchia declared, happy with all departments of his game. There were three putts at the third and a missed green at the seventeenth, both costing him shots, but against that six

Wayne Grady felt he was playing 'smart golf' in taking a two-stroke lead.

birdies, two of which he holed from off the green, at the first with his putter and at the fifth with a chip.

Norman, who has become a much slower player these days, was urged to get a move on without it being an official warning. He thought they just happened to be a slow group, each in turn getting into trouble. Nevertheless, a 70 kept him in the picture and he was more pleased with his putting, even if he did not hole a lot, than with some rather sloppy play around the turn.

What saved Norman from obscurity was his finish, for he made birdies at both the sixteenth and seventeenth, his two at the latter the result of a putt of some ten yards. 'The last four or five holes I played really, well,' said Norman, 'and that was when I had to.' Perhaps it was then that he first began to lick his lips.

There was, however, less sign of Faldo, who was acutely disappointed with a second 71. He knew he had to get in a low score to get into contention and it just did not happen, any more than it did with a lack-lustre Ballesteros. However, Faldo could have been unsettled by an unfortunate accident at the fourth hole.

Having driven into a bunker, he played out and then hit a four wood into the crowd to the right of the green. So too did Tateo (Jet) Ozaki, one of his partners, and one of the balls hit a woman spectator a fearful blow on the head. Doctors in the crowd gave first aid, an ambulance was summoned, and the police further dramatized the situation by issuing a statement declaring that the woman's name was being withheld 'until relatives had been informed'.

This suggested the worst. In fact, Mrs Anne Welsh, of Dumfries, regained consciousness in hospital and was released from hospital the following day, if not none the worse, certainly in better shape than had at one time been inferred.

After a delay, the hole cost Faldo a six and though he came back with an immediate birdie, it was all rather hard work, hopes reviving with successive birdies at the fourteenth and fifteenth, but then a two iron wide of the seventeenth green, from where there is almost no way of getting down in two.

Clark had the longest run of birdies he could remember – five from the eleventh – in his 68 but generally it was not as notable a day for the Europeans as it was for one Japanese family. Jet, Naomichi (Joe) and Masashi (Jumbo) Ozaki all qualified for the last thirty-six holes; and the last time three brothers did that must have been in the days of the Whitcombes, Charles, Reg and Ernest, many moons ago in the 1930s.

American Steve Pate (right) was joint seventh, but Ian Woosnam was 11 strokes off the lead after 36 holes.

(Clockwise from top left): Roger Chapman recovered from a bad start, Eduardo Romero was having another good Open performance, five-times Open champion Tom Watson was a favourite of the crowds, Howard Clark returned a second-round 68, David Feherty raised Irish hopes, Mark James was only four shots behind, three Japanese brothers – Masashi, Tateo and (not pictured) Naomichi Ozaki – made the 36-hole cut.

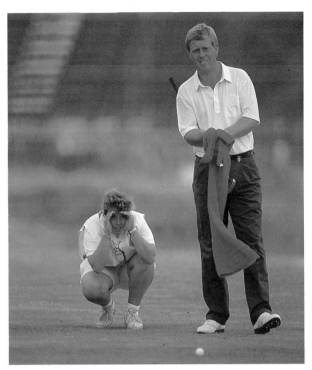

SECOND ROUND RESULTS

HOLE	1	2	3	4	5	6	7	8	9	10	11	12	13	14	15	16	17	18	TOTAL
PAR	4	4	4	5	3	5	4	3	4	4	5	4	4	3	4	5	3	4	TOTAL
Wayne Grady	4	3	4	5	2	5	3	2	5	3	4	4	4	3	4	5	3	4	67-135
Payne Stewart	4	3	4	4	3	3	4	3	4	4	4	4	2	5	4	3	3		65-137
Tom Watson	4	3	4	5	3	4	4	3	4	4	4	3	5	3	4	3	3	5	68-137
Eduardo Romero	5	5	4	5	3	4	4	2	4	4	4	3	4	3	4	5	3	4	70-138
David Feherty	3	4	4	4	2	4	4	2	4	4	4	4	3	3	4	6	3	5	67-138
Wayne Stephens	4	4	4	4	3	4	4	4	5	3	5	4	5	5	3	4	3	4	72-138
Derrick Cooper	4	4	4	4	4	5	4	3	4	4	5	4	3	3	4	4	4	3	70-139
Greg Norman	3	4	4	4	4	5	4	3	5	4	4	4	5	3	4	4	2	4	70-139
Steve Pate	4	4	4	4	3	5	4	3	4	5	4	4	4	3	4	4	3	4	70-139
Mark James	4	4	4	4	3	5	4	2	4	4	5	4	4	3	4	4	3	5	70-139
Scott Simpson	3	3	4	4	3	5	5	2	5	5	4	3	4	3	3	4	3	3	66-139
Mark McCumber	4	3	5	4	4	4	5	2	3	4	4	4	4	2	4	4	4	4	68-139
Mark Calcavecchia	3	4	5	4	2	5	3	3	4	4	5	4	3	3	3	4	4	4	68-139
Fred Couples	4	4	5	5	3	5	5	3	4	4	4	3	3	2	4	5	3	5	71-139

HOLE SUMMARY

HOLE	PAR	EAGLES	BIRDIES	PARS	BOGEYS	HIGHER	RANK	AVERAGE
1	4	0	23	116	16	1	13	3.97
2	4	1	26	95	32	2	10	4.05
3	4	0	20	114	19	3	11	4.04
4	5	2	42	85	25	2	16	4.89
5	3	0	18	93	40	5	4	3.21
6	5	2	34	99	17	4	14	4.92
7	4	0	23	97	32	4	9	4.12
8	3	0	36	97	18	5	15	2.95
9	4	0	10	103	31	12	2	4.31
OUT	36	5	232	899	230	38		36.46
10	4	0	11	91	49	5	2	4.31
11	5	3	88	47	14	4	18	4.54
12	4	0	25	89	29	13	5	4.22
13	4	0	16	100	36	4	7	4.18
14	3	0	26	102	27	1	12	3.02
15	4	0	10	106	38	2	6	4.21
16	5	1	45	99	11	0	17	4.77
17	3	0	10	101	42	3	1	3.24
18	4	0	18	97	39	2	8	4.16
IN	36	4	249	832	285	34		36.65
TOTAL	72	9	481	1731	515	72		73.11

Australia's Wayne Grady believed his hard work was beginning to pay off.

Players Below Par	49
Players At Par	14
Players Above Par	93

LOW SCORES

Low First Nine	Richard Boxall	31
	David Feherty	31
Low Second Nine	Michael Allen	32
	Emmanuel Dussart	32
	Scott Simpson	32
Low Round	Payne Stewart	65

Middle rounds of 65, 69 got colourful Payne Stewart into the race for the championship.

DAY

3

THE LEADERS
KEEP AN EVEN PACE

BY MICHAEL WILLIAMS

About the only thing that caught fire on the third day of the Open Championship was the golf course. With the grass tinder dry, a discarded cigarette or broken piece of glass with the sun concentrating the heat were all that were necessary to get a blaze going. The prompt arrival of the fire brigade and a certain amount of smoke beside the ninth fairway were no more than interesting diversions before the principals took the stage.

Another curiosity was that the general shape of things did not alter very much, nobody breaking away. It was not unlike a 1,500-metre race as the runners approached the bell for the fourth and last lap, the leaders all keeping an even pace, pretty well shoulder to shoulder with only Wayne Stephens, that unexpected first round pace-setter, and Eduardo Romero beginning to flag. Having shared fourth place after two rounds, both dropped back, Romero with a 75 and Stephens with a 76. they had had their moments.

What may have surprised some was that Wayne Grady, of Australia, kept a yard, as it were, ahead with a 69 to now stand twelve under par for the fifty-four holes. Significantly, or so it seemed, however, Tom Watson closed up on him with a 68 to be eleven under, a stroke ahead of another American, Payne Stewart, who had a 69.

Right behind him came a group of three, two Americans again in Mark Calcavecchia, who had a second successive 68, and Fred Couples, who came back with a similar score; and also the Irishman, David Feherty, still very much hanging on with a 69. A growing United States presence was also underlined as Paul Azinger sprinted up with a 67 to move alongside Jodie Mudd, who was round in 68.

One name was of course conspicuous by its absence

in all this, and that was Greg Norman. He had drifted back into the pack with a 72, now one of ten players on 211, seven strokes off the lead, with twelve players ahead of him. Hardly surprisingly therefore Norman's price with the bookmakers drifted back from the nine-to-two joint favourite he had been at the start of the day with Watson to twenty-five-to-one.

Watson therefore became favourite on his own at seven-to-four, a sentiment certainly shared by the Scottish crowd who greeted his every step on this gloriously hot and sunlit afternoon as if he was one of their own. Grady was second favourite at nine-to-two, Stewart eleven-to-two, Calcavecchia and Couples both eight-to-one. Feherty and Jose-Maria Olazabal, who had had a 69 to draw level with Mark McCumber (70) and Steve Pate (70) for a share of ninth place, were regarded as best of the European bets, both sixteen-to-one.

Considering such ideal conditions, the links glistening in the sunlight and the bathers wallowing in the sea, it was surprising nobody took greater advantage, for early on there was a 66 from Larry Mize, who came home in 32 and remarking how easily the course was playing, giving him the chance to be aggressive. 'You can score but you have to hit the ball well,' he said. There was a 67 from Mark Davis, a young Essex professional who is beginning to make a mark on the European circuit despite suffering from diabetes, and another from Roger Chapman, who made eagle-threes at both the fourth and sixth holes.

This had also been the last chance for Nick Faldo to pick himself up off the floor and a buzz swept the course when the score-boards revealed that he had made birdies at the fourth, sixth, eighth and ninth. Out in 32, Faldo was six under par for the championship and with the leaders not yet launched, he was technically only three strokes off the lead.

Was this then his move at long last? Alas, no. He got a flier with an eight iron out of the rough at the tenth, chipped to eight feet and missed the putt. There was a birdie to counter at the eleventh, but then another, and even shorter, putt missed at the twelfth as again he missed the green. At once he lost confidence in his swing, unable to find the right position in the takeaway. Another shot went at the last and though a 70 was his best round yet, Faldo declared himself 'fed up'.

Less surprisingly, there was nothing either from Sandy Lyle, who returned a 71. 'I'm hitting three bad shots a round and they are costing me dearly,' he admitted afterwards. At one over par for the fifty-four holes, he was a long way from where he had been when he won the championship at Royal St George's in 1984.

Grady, on the other hand, was nearer than ever to the most cherished prize in golf. He was also much more aware of it than when he led after thirty-six holes, leaving the course soon after lunch and not returning. He claimed to have read the morning paper for fifteen minutes before discovering that he was still ahead. This is not quite as remarkable as it may seem. The top golfers tend to look at a tournament or championship as a whole and not at the three segments that shape it before the final round. They take stock only when the last lap is about to begin.

For nine holes Grady made no progress against par, and when he did at last get a birdie at the tenth, it was due only to his holing a chip. Then he chipped close for another birdie at the eleventh and progressed serenely on his way until the fourteenth, where he was bunkered under the lip. From there he could not even go for the flag and deliberately played well away from it, forty feet or more. Clearly Grady was thinking only of cutting his losses, and it was a huge bonus for him when he then sank the putt to save his par.

Having made good his escape, Grady pitched dead for a birdie-four at the sixteenth and then salvaged another par at the seventeenth, which was ultimately

to rank as Royal Troon's most difficult hole against par. 'I got out of the round very well,' he admitted. 'I hit my irons poorly, which was disappointing, because I had been hitting them well. I think I maybe got a bit short and quick. My chipping and putting made up for it and it was important that I made a good score out of a so-so round. That's what it is all about.'

It was clearly also encouraging to him that he had played the back nine so well, in 33. This was where the championship was going to be decided and it was unlikely that tomorrow he would get nothing out of the front nine. All things considered, Grady had had something of a scrape but got away with it.

However there was no doubt as to who was now the crowd's favourite, and that was Watson, wearing somewhat incongruously in the hot sun a tweed cap as if in recognition of his Scottish surroundings. One was tempted to wonder whether he even considered donning a kilt as well!

Furthermore this 68 by Watson had less of the charmed life about it that so featured the same score he had made the previous day. This was a well-put-together round of golf that wobbled only towards the end when at the fifteenth, sixteenth and eighteenth he found himself in difficulties from which he extricated himself only by dint of a reviving short game.

At the fifteenth, he was in the left rough off the tee but in the end saved his par with a glorious little pitch to within inches of the hole. Then, at the sixteenth, where he played for position and relied on an accurate pitch for his birdie four, Watson instead pushed the ball a fraction and went into one of the bunkers on the right, close to the pin. He had little room with which to 'work' the ball, could only get it to fifteen feet but then, glory be, holed it for his par. Then, at the last, he was left chipping again from wide of the green, but again did it with all the flamboyance of former years.

Earlier Watson had had just the start he was looking for, with a birdie at the first from fifteen feet, two tricky putts at the next two holes safely bottled for pars and then another five-yarder sunk at the fourth for a birdie. Presently he was through the turn in 34, which he repeated coming home with birdies at the eleventh (two putts) and more impressively down the hog's back of a thirteenth fairway with a drive and seven iron to eight feet.

'It's nice to be in the hunt,' said Watson. 'I was nervous at first but very calm on the back side. A lot of good things are happening and I cannot wait for tomorrow to put it to the test again. A couple of faults came together and organized my thoughts about the swing, but I'm not concentrating too much on the mechanics, just the feel.'

He recognized however that this was a very tame Royal Troon and that it was this which had probably helped him to get into contention, in that he doubted he had seen as much of the fairways as some of the leaders. 'The course is giving away a lot this year, but it will take a lot back in the future,' added Watson, who felt that the five Open championships he had already won 'would not hurt. When you win on a course, it's easier to win the second time because you have the same feeling. I have never forgotten the feeling I had in 1982.'

Nor was Watson by any means the only man who was happy with the way things were shaping. So too was Stewart, whose 69 was immaculately compiled since he hit seventeen greens in regulation, the only one he missed being the short fourteenth, which consequently cost him a four. If this was disappointing, it was not as irritating as the sixth hole had been. Two great shots, the second with a three wood, had raised a big cheer as his ball climbed the slope, leaving him with a putt for an eagle. Having missed it, Stewart then missed the one back as well from less than a yard.

Otherwise, it was all very orderly golf, Stewart's four birdies coming at the fourth, where he chipped close from the side of the green; the ninth, where he sank a putt of some twenty feet; the eleventh, where his chip for an eagle-three brushed the hole; and most impressively at the seventeenth, where he sank a putt of thirty feet or more for a two.

In fact, putting was the one department of Stewart's game that he felt was lacking. He was not always getting up to the hole with his approaches and if he had, he thought he could have shot a 62. 'I like

my position a lot,' he said. 'It is the best I have been in a major but tomorrow is the day you win and that is what I am going to try to do.'

It would not, I think, be an exaggeration to say that little attention was still being paid to Calcavecchia, though a second successive 68 had kept him very much in the picture, sharing now fourth place with Couples and Feherty, all of them three strokes behind. Calcavecchia's Press interview was fairly brief and centred mostly on his putting, where he felt there was also room for improvement.

He had missed from inside a yard at the third for a birdie and there were a couple of others he thought he should have holed but did not. In fact he had been using the same club for some six weeks, one of eight Answer putters sent to him by an admirer in Texas. He had chosen three and this was one of them.

What Calcavecchia did regret was leaving out of his bag his three iron. Inevitably this was just the club he needed at the seventeenth. Instead he had to use a two iron, hooked it left and then took four more to get down from below the bank. 'I think tomorrow I will leave the one iron out,' mused the American.

This four at the short seventeenth was not the only shot he dropped. Another had slipped away with a six at the fourth, which must have felt more like a double bogey than a bogey. However, he quickly made up for it with twos at the fifth and eighth and in between a four at the long sixth, which he reached in two.

Out in 34, Calcavecchia proceeded to exchange a birdie at the eleventh for a bogey at the twelfth before cutting loose with three birdies in his next four holes. Six irons at the thirteenth and fourteenth set him up for a three and then a two, while at the sixteenth he hit a driver just short and then flipped a sand wedge to twelve inches or so.

Feherty, it might be true to say, was surprising a lot of people by the manner in which he was still 'hanging in there', now with a 69, the first half of which was much less eventful than the second. The Ulsterman sank two fifteen-foot putts on the second and fourth greens for birdies and otherwise played straightforward par golf; a man on terms with himself.

With further birdies at the eleventh, which was

(Clockwise from top left): Tom Kite described the course as 'defenceless' after he returned a 67, and fellow-American Larry Mize returned a 66, Jack Nicklaus again had Jimmy Dickinson as his caddy, and Johnny Miller relied on his son.

Payne Stewart puts an arm around Wayne Grady after both returned 69s in the third round.

a conventional two-putt affair, and at the twelfth, which was entirely unconventional since it was the result of the huge putt of some fifty feet, Feherty was ten under par in total and poised. However it became much more of a struggle after that, with three putts from a long way at the thirteenth and then a flurry of chips and single putts through the next four holes, all of them to save par.

Since he had no previous experience of being so closely involved in a major championship, Feherty was well pleased with the way his game had stood up. It was only the second time he had got through to the last two rounds of the Open, Muirfield in 1987 being the other, but as he had been hitting the ball well for several weeks, he had brought his game with him and had also, as he put it, got 'good visualization'. This is the art of immediately 'seeing the shot' that has to be played and then having the confidence to play it.

Couples, who is utterly 'sold' on links golf, came back into the picture with a 68 that could so easily have been better. Though he made birdies at both the second and fourth, he felt he could have done the same at the first and third as well. Indeed almost anything might have happened over those first nine holes, though only one more birdie was made, a two at the eighth.

Conversely, on the back nine Couples seldom got the ball near the flag, though he did make fours at the two par fives, holing from six yards at the sixteenth. But he messed up his drive at the last and was never looking at better than a five.

Azinger had a model round that could easily have been better than a 67. Having gone out in 34 he was looking at birdies from that teasing fifteen-foot range at the tenth, thirteenth, fourteenth and fifteenth holes without sinking one of them. Then he did at last get one in at the sixteenth, followed with another at the seventeenth, but ironically missed from half the distance at the eighteenth.

Mudd, Azinger's partner, was only one shot worse with a 68. It was his first Open and he was disconcerted by the attention of photographers, particularly over the early holes. He had never expected such perfect weather, after having watched other Opens on television, with everyone muffled up in waterproofs, but with the help of a local caddy he had quickly adjusted to the fastest course on which he had ever played.

Meanwhile Norman, nicely poised at two under par for the first ten holes, proceeded to drop strokes at three of the remaining eight, relieved only by a two at the seventeenth. Back in 38 for a 72, he had, it seemed, lost all contact with the leaders. How wrong that assumption proved to be.

Said Wayne Grady of maintaining his lead, 'I did what I had to do.'

Tom Watson was in an ideal position after 54 holes, one stroke off the lead.

THIRD ROUND RESULTS

HOLE	1	2	3	4	5	6	7	8	9	10	11	12	13	14	15	16	17	18	
PAR	4	4	4	5	3	5	4	3	4	4	5	4	4	3	4	5	3	4	TOTAL
Wayne Grady	4	4	4	5	3	5	4	3	4	3	4	4	4	3	4	4	3	4	69-204
Tom Watson	3	4	4	4	3	5	4	3	4	4	4	4	3	3	4	5	3	4	68-205
Payne Stewart	4	4	4	4	3	5	4	3	3	4	4	4	4	4	4	5	2	4	69-206
Fred Couples	4	3	4	4	3	5	4	2	4	4	4	4	3	4	4	4	3	5	68-207
Mark Calcavecchia	4	4	4	6	2	4	4	2	4	4	4	5	3	2	4	4	4	4	68-207
David Feherty	4	3	4	4	3	5	4	3	4	4	4	3	5	3	4	5	3	4	69-207
Paul Azinger	4	3	4	4	3	5	4	3	4	4	4	4	4	3	4	4	2	4	67-208
Jodie Mudd	4	4	4	4	3	4	3	2	4	4	4	4	5	3	4	5	3	4	68-208
Jose-Maria Olazabal	5	3	3	5	2	6	4	3	4	4	4	4	4	3	4	4	3	4	69-209
Mark McCumber	4	4	4	4	3	5	4	3	4	4	5	4	4	3	4	5	3	3	70-209
Steve Pate	4	4	5	4	4	4	4	2	4	4	4	4	4	3	4	5	3	4	70-209
Mark James	4	4	4	4	5	5	5	2	4	4	4	4	4	2	4	5	3	4	71-210
Greg Norman	4	4	4	4	3	4	3	4	4	4	6	5	4	3	4	5	2	5	72-211

HOLE SUMMARY

HOLE	PAR	EAGLES	BIRDIES	PARS	BOGEYS	HIGHER	RANK	AVERAGE
1	4	0	11	56	13	0	9	4.03
2	4	1	15	54	8	2	11	3.95
3	4	0	12	62	6	0	12	3.93
4	5	4	39	34	3	0	18	4.45
5	3	0	7	53	17	3	3	3.20
6	5	1	28	42	8	1	16	4.75
7	4	0	17	55	7	1	13	3.90
8	3	0	20	50	10	0	15	2.88
9	4	0	7	57	15	1	7	4.13
OUT	36	6	156	463	87	8		35.22
10	4	0	5	53	19	3	4	4.25
11	5	3	43	29	4	1	17	4.46
12	4	0	4	60	14	2	6	4.18
13	4	0	6	58	16	0	7	4.13
14	3	0	12	58	10	0	10	2.98
15	4	0	2	56	20	2	2	4.28
16	5	1	21	50	7	1	14	4.83
17	3	0	7	51	19	3	1	3.23
18	4	0	9	51	17	3	5	4.19
IN	36	4	109	466	126	15		36.53
TOTAL	72	10	265	929	213	23		71.75

American Jodie Mudd had middle rounds of 67, 68 and eventually placed fifth.

Players Below Par	37
Players At Par	9
Players Above Par	34

LOW SCORES		
Low First Nine	Roger Chapman	32
	Nick Faldo	32
	Tom Kite	32
	Jodie Mudd	32
Low Second Nine	Larry Mize	32
Low Round	Larry Mize	66

After leading for two rounds, Wayne Grady could not produce the pars he needed on the last two holes.

DAY

4

CALCAVECCHIA'S DRAMATIC FINISH

BY MICHAEL WILLIAMS

On the eve of the Open Championship's final round, Mark Calcavecchia headed back to Ayr, where he was staying at the Caledonian Hotel. He was three strokes off the lead but his thoughts were many miles from Royal Troon. He took the lift to his room and telephoned his home in West Palm Beach, Florida, where it was early afternoon. His wife, Sheryl, answered and the sound of her reassuring voice was all that Calcavecchia wanted to hear.

With the birth of their first child imminent, it had been worrying him that she might have gone into labour. If she had, her husband was fully prepared to catch the first available flight back to the States and, not to put too fine a point on it, 'to blazes with the last round of the Open Championship.' Whether as sensible a person as Sheryl would have stood for that was another matter. There are strong grounds for believing that she would not. At all events, Calcavecchia put the phone down with a sense of relief. After an early night and a good night's sleep, he decided that he would go for a run in the morning.

That same Saturday evening Greg Norman booked a table for four at the Marine Hotel, Troon, which is within a wedge of the eighteenth green. He and his wife were dining with their close friends, the Mansells, Nigel that is of motor racing distinction. Greg has a love of cars that is matched only by Nigel's devotion to golf. Nigel, from within the ropes, had walked every step of the way during Greg's third round, a disappointing 72 that left him seven strokes off the lead.

A few tables away were the Nicklauses and, as they left the restaurant, Jack paused to wish Greg the best of luck in the last round. If the King had had the power to have named his successor, there is little doubt that Nicklaus would have nominated Norman; and he had a word of advice, disappointed

to have seen the Australian drop a shot at the eighteenth that afternoon because of what he felt was too much aggression. 'Put more brain into your game,' Nicklaus said.

Some minutes later the Floyds passed by, Raymond reminding Norman of the low score he would have to shoot but warning him 'not to force it'. Tom Weiskopf, who had won the Open at Royal Troon in 1973 and had stayed on despite missing the cut, added more words of wisdom. 'Put a little finesse into your game,' he urged. Norman was not therefore short of advice as he retired to bed. There he had a dream: of three threes.

In a small house in Troon, Wayne Grady, the championship leader for the past two days, was settling down for a quiet evening with his wife, Lyn, two-year-old Samantha and a couple of friends. It had been a bit cramped all week but Grady, typically, had said he would sleep on the sofa, and on the sofa he slept.

Thus in their separate ways did three golfers, two of them Australian and the other American, prepare themselves for one of the most dramatic final afternoons in the history of the Open, producing as it did the first play-off since 1975, the first three-man play-off and the first to be played over only four holes. When, fourteen years earlier, Tom Watson had beaten Jack Newton at Carnoustie, it was played over eighteen holes while as recently as 1963 Bob Charles played off against Phil Rodgers over thirty-six holes at Royal Lytham.

This latest shortening of the play-off was introduced by the R & A in 1985, it being regarded as a compromise between a full round of golf and the alternative of sudden death, which would only come into operation if the players were still tied. Both the Masters and the American PGA Championship are now decided if necessary by sudden death, which leaves only the US Open faithful to the eighteen hole play-off.

Oddly enough, the format was not known by Calcavecchia when he stepped on to the first tee, having tied with Norman and Grady at a thirteen-under-par total of 275, for he believed it was to have been sudden death. Fortunately for him it was not, for otherwise the championship could (one hesitates to say 'would' under different circumstances) have gone to other hands. Instead the title went to Calcavecchia, the first American winner since Tom Watson in 1983. But behind the tears of triumph lay as well two stories of heart-break as Norman, not for the first time, and Grady experienced the emptiness of being so tantalizingly near and yet so far.

Already Norman had lost in 1984 a play-off for the US Open against Fuzzy Zoeller as well as a play-off for the 1987 Masters against Larry Mize. He had lost, too, the 1986 American PGA when Bob Tway holed from a bunker at the last hole and he had twice, including this year, taken five at the eighteenth in the Masters when a four would have got him into a play-off.

With seven strokes to make up, Norman's cause seemed hopeless but now, as he took the long walk from the practice ground on the adjacent Portland course, crossed the road behind the Marine Hotel and walked through the R & A compound to the first tee an hour and a half before the leaders, he remembered that dream he had had of three threes. He knew this was the moment when he had to throw caution to the wind.

Norman started not only with those three threes but six consecutive birdies. By the time he was striding to the seventh tee, he was eleven under par for the championship and only a stroke behind Grady, who had not yet driven off. Immediately one was put in mind of Johnny Miller, six behind going into the last round of the 1973 US Open, beginning with four successive birdies en route to a 63 and one of the most remarkable victories the game has known.

There are few greater sights than Norman, tall and lean with his fair hair almost flashing in the sunlight, and it was possible to monitor his progress down the course as at regular intervals a roar would go up to greet his latest birdie. As soon as, on the first tee, he reached for his driver, his intentions were as obvious as the set of his jaw.

There followed: a pitch to seven feet at the first, a sand wedge to fifteen feet at the second, a wedge to two feet at the third (after laying up short of the ditch with a two iron), a drive, four iron and two putts at the fourth, a sand iron to forty-five feet at the fifth, a drive, three wood left and then the 'pitch of my life' to four feet at the sixth. There seemed no holding him.

A 63 was what Norman had in mind, but at the Postage Stamp eighth, he pitched high up in the mound on the left, his ball bounced down into the bunker and he took four. Out in 31, Norman gathered himself again. He reached the eleventh with a drive and five iron and two-putted for a birdie; he hit a seven iron thirty-five feet away at the twelfth and holed that putt. More were still needed, but he got nothing out of the thirteenth, fourteenth or fifteenth, pars each time.

At the sixteenth he laid up short of the burn with a two iron and had 277 yards left to the flag. All the world seemed to hold its breath as, after lengthy deliberation, Norman reached for his driver. This was the moment and he hit a glorious stroke, picking the ball clean and as straight as a die between the bunkers and six yards beyond the flag. It would have been a crowning moment had he sunk the putt for an eagle. Instead his ball slipped by.

However, if this was a chance lost, Norman had cause to be thankful at the seventeenth, where he looked as if he was about to drop a shot but instead retrieved a three by deliberately blading with the leading edge of his sand wedge and holing it to save par. Minutes later he was reducing the eighteenth, 452 yards, to a drive and nine iron, two-putting for a four, and had set a course record of 64. On 275 he had set the target and could only sit and wait.

An hour and a half behind, Grady had begun impressively, partnered by Watson. Both made birdies at the first, Grady almost holing his second shot, Watson by virtue of a putt of fifteen feet or so after a skilful second shot from a difficult sandy lie in the rough. Little chips and single putts saw Grady safely through the next two holes and then he reached the fourth with two solid shots and two-putted for a second birdie.

It was on this same hole that Watson's challenge for his sixth Open began to fade. He had driven into the rough on the left but had a good lie, good enough anyway to take a wood for his second. It came out low, caught a small hump and 'killed' the shot. Watson made his par safely enough but when Grady then holed for a two at the fifth, the difference between them was three strokes.

Grady's first mistake was to miss the ninth green and then miss a putt of not much more than a yard to save par. Even so, he was out in 34 and still clear on his own. With a birdie at the twelfth, the Australian still had two strokes in hand from Norman, who had by then finished and was taking a telephone call of congratulation from the Australian Prime Minister, Bob Hawke.

Thirty-five minutes ahead of Grady was Calcavecchia, who earlier that morning had gone on a three-and-a-half mile run. All he could think about as he pounded along was what it would be like to win the Open, of how he had tried too hard when well-placed in the Canadian and Greater Hartford Opens and how he should this time, simply 'let himself go'.

Yet it was not happening. He had not made as much of the outward half (35) as he had hoped and now things began to take a turn for the worse. Only a great chip helped to save par at the tenth, while what happened at the next two holes, he was later to describe as 'a miracle of God'.

He got into all sorts of trouble down the eleventh, hacking around in the rough, tangling with a prickly gorse bush and finally scrambling his way on to the green in four and then of all things holing a putt of forty feet to save par. Even better was to follow. Again he was in trouble from the tee at the twelfth, next in the gallery left of the green, high up on a grassy bank. Even to have saved par would have been a bonus. Instead Calcavecchia lofted his little pitch, it hit the flagstick and dropped straight into the hole without even bouncing. Birdie!

'Those things just do not ordinarily happen,' said Calcavecchia afterwards. 'I just think everything went my way.' But a golfer must also make the most of his luck, and Calcavecchia certainly made the most of his. He did not falter over the next three holes and at the sixteenth, like Norman, ripped a driver off the fairway to thirty feet and two-putted for a birdie. Now twelve under par, he needed one more birdie to catch Norman.

It came at the last, a glorious eight iron from 161 yards to four feet, and there was Calcavecchia holing out for a three and a 68 to draw level with Norman and join him in the anxious wait to see whether Grady could overtake them. Unlike Nick Price seven years earlier, it was not the thirteenth and fifteenth holes that undid the Australian, but instead the fourteenth, where he took three putts. His lead was down to a single stroke and he did not get the cushion he needed at the sixteenth either, just missing for a birdie.

Two pars at the finish would have done it but, like Price seven years earlier, Grady missed the seventeenth green, bunkered right. He came out well but the putt somehow escaped the hole and now the Australian, having led on his own for two days, needed a par even to tie. From the back fringe, he chipped as surely as ever and there was the three-way tie, the first in Open history.

What happened next, as the crowds dashed for vantage points down the first, second, seventeenth and eighteenth holes will surely stand alongside the gathering collection of Norman calamities. Gathering himself for one last supreme effort he made birdie threes at both the first (where many spectators, thinking it was a sudden-death play-off, acclaimed him as champion) and second holes, distancing himself immediately from Grady but not quite from Calcavecchia, who had preceded him into the hole for a three at the second.

At this point Norman had played twenty consecutive holes in 70 strokes and when, with the honour, he struck a three iron straight and true to the seventeenth, it seemed for all the world as if nothing could now stop him. If anything Norman struck the ball too well, for it came to rest against the fringe

Greg Norman's brilliant final day started with six birdies in succession, but ended in disappointment at the 18th in the play-off.

Irishman David Feherty held up well to the pressure and was joint sixth.

at the back of the green. It was a tricky rather than difficult shot and Norman elected to chip with his wedge when he might have putted or even, as when he last visited this green, bladed the ball again. His shot was too strong and he missed the putt. Grady also took four but Calcavecchia made a cast-iron three and was back in a tie, both he and Norman one under for the first three holes of the play-off, one to play.

When Calcavecchia cut his drive on the last hole, opportunity beckoned for Norman once again. Out came his driver and he put every last ounce into it, so much so that the ball never stopped running, bouncing and hopping along until it rolled into a bunker so far down the fairway that he never for a moment believed he could reach it. Furthermore it was up against the face.

Waiting now to play an impossible shot if he was to reach the green, Norman's heart can only have sunk as Calcavecchia, so far back that he needed now a five iron as opposed to an eight before, hit another stunning shot seven feet short of the flag.

Norman's recovery caught the face of the bunker, flew high into the air and dropped in another bunker on the other side of the fairway. From there, his cause hopeless, he went out of bounds and there was no point in playing on. It remained only for Calcavecchia to go through the formality of holing his putt for a three he did not need but which, like a true champion, he did.

At twenty-nine, Calcavecchia represents the new generation of American golfers, one who takes such pride in his country that all season he had been declaring that his top-most priority had been to be a member of the team which regains the Ryder Cup. No one, he believes, can count on winning major championships.

There were fourteen Americans in the top thirty, Watson fourth after a 72 for 277, two behind the three leaders. A stroke behind him came Jodie Mudd (70), followed by Fred Couples (72) together with Europe's top player, David Feherty, also 72.

Nick Faldo, the favourite before a ball had been struck on the Thursday, improved again with a 69 but equal eleventh was to him a severe disappoint-

ment. He said he was going fishing. Had it been a lake two players might have considered jumping into it. Bernhard Langer finished last and Severiano Ballesteros, the defending champion, third last. What a difference twelve months can make.

Nevertheless, this had been a week for some of the lowest scoring in the history of the Open Championship. Starting with those forty-one scores below par in the first round, the contestants proceeded to return a total of 151 scores below par, out of 432 rounds played, which was an average of better than one score out of three. Because par at the championship venues varies from 70 to 72, the only record of this sort is for rounds below 70. There were seventy-two rounds below 70, which was a record, four more than were recorded at Royal Birkdale in 1983.

Had Grady and Watson scored below 70 in the fourth round, they would have been the first in the history of the championship to have all four rounds under 70. The final results had Calcavecchia, Norman, Grady and Watson with three rounds under 70, bringing to twelve the number of contestants to have done so in the history of the championship.

Payne Stewart could manage only a 74 on the last day for joint eighth place.

Tom Watson, in the company of
Wayne Grady, saw his challenge
fade after four holes, leaving
Grady to play-off with Mark
Calcavecchia and Greg Norman.

Dramatic gestures became
common place as Greg Norman
scored 11 birdies in 20 holes.

FOURTH ROUND RESULTS

HOLE	1	2	3	4	5	6	7	8	9	10	11	12	13	14	15	16	17	18	
PAR	4	4	4	5	3	5	4	3	4	4	5	4	4	3	4	5	3	4	TOTAL
Mark Calcavecchia	4	3	4	4	3	5	5	3	4	4	5	3	4	3	4	4	3	3	68-275
Greg Norman	3	3	3	4	2	4	4	4	4	4	4	3	4	3	4	4	3	4	64-275
Wayne Grady	3	4	4	4	2	5	4	3	5	4	5	3	4	4	4	5	4	4	71-275
Tom Watson	3	4	4	5	3	4	5	3	5	5	4	4	4	3	4	5	3	4	72-277
Jodie Mudd	3	3	4	5	3	4	4	3	4	4	4	4	4	4	4	5	4	4	70-278
David Feherty	3	4	4	5	4	4	4	3	4	4	4	5	4	4	5	4	3	4	72-279
Fred Couples	4	5	4	6	3	6	3	4	5	5	5	3	4	3	3	4	2	3	72-279
Eduardo Romero	4	4	4	5	3	4	3	2	4	4	4	3	4	3	4	5	3	4	67-280
Paul Azinger	4	5	5	4	3	5	4	2	4	4	4	4	4	3	4	5	3	5	72-280
Payne Stewart	4	4	3	5	3	4	4	4	6	4	4	4	3	4	6	4	3	5	74-280
Mark McNulty	4	4	4	4	2	4	4	3	4	4	4	4	5	4	3	4	2	3	66-281
Nick Faldo	3	4	4	4	2	4	4	3	5	4	4	4	5	2	5	5	3	4	69-281

HOLE SUMMARY

HOLE	PAR	EAGLES	BIRDIES	PARS	BOGEYS	HIGHER	RANK	AVERAGE
1	4	0	13	58	9	0	14	3.95
2	4	0	12	57	11	0	12	3.99
3	4	0	6	61	13	0	11	4.09
4	5	3	41	32	3	1	18	4.48
5	3	0	11	53	15	1	10	3.08
6	5	1	30	39	7	3	15	4.78
7	4	0	12	57	11	0	12	3.99
8	3	0	12	48	20	0	8	3.10
9	4	0	5	51	19	5	5	4.33
OUT	36	4	142	456	108	10		35.79
10	4	0	3	49	24	4	2	4.39
11	5	2	41	28	6	3	17	4.60
12	4	0	11	49	19	1	9	4.13
13	4	0	4	55	17	4	7	4.26
14	3	0	4	56	20	0	6	3.20
15	4	0	6	43	27	4	3	4.36
16	5	0	22	54	4	0	15	4.78
17	3	0	5	47	24	4	1	3.34
18	4	0	5	50	19	6	4	4.35
IN	36	2	101	431	160	26		37.41
TOTAL	72	6	243	887	268	36		73.20

			LOW SCORES		
Players Below Par	24				
Players At Par	13	Low First Nine	Brian Marchbank	30	
Players Above Par	43	Low Second Nine	Fred Couples	32	
		Low Round	Greg Norman	64	

CHAMPIONSHIP HOLE SUMMARY

HOLE	PAR	EAGLES	BIRDIES	PARS	BOGEYS	HIGHER	RANK	AVERAGE
1	4	0	60	343	67	2	13	4.02
2	4	2	64	316	85	5	11	4.06
3	4	0	58	345	63	6	12	4.04
4	5	16	172	231	50	3	17	4.69
5	3	0	53	298	110	11	6	3.17
6	5	8	131	262	58	13	15	4.87
7	4	0	74	305	82	11	10	4.07
8	3	0	96	293	73	10	14	3.00
9	4	0	36	312	101	23	4	4.25
OUT	36	26	744	2705	689	84		36.17
10	4	0	29	284	143	16	2	4.31
11	5	10	243	169	38	12	18	4.58
12	4	0	54	301	97	20	8	4.18
13	4	0	41	307	115	9	7	4.19
14	3	0	61	323	86	2	9	3.06
15	4	0	39	292	124	17	3	4.26
16	5	3	126	299	43	1	16	4.82
17	3	0	30	295	135	12	1	3.27
18	4	0	42	300	113	17	5	4.23
IN	36	13	665	2570	894	106		36.90
TOTAL	72	39	1409	5275	1583	190		73.07

	FIRST ROUND	SECOND ROUND	THIRD ROUND	FOURTH ROUND	TOTAL
Players Below Par	41	49	37	24	151
Players At Par	19	14	9	13	55
Players Above Par	96	93	34	43	266

ATTENDANCE

PRACTICE ROUNDS	30,604
FIRST ROUND	27,825
SECOND ROUND	33,458
THIRD ROUND	34,794
FOURTH ROUND	33,958
TOTAL	160,639

COMMENTARY

THE BOY FROM LAUREL, NEBRASKA

BY MARINO PARASCENZO

In Nebraska, state law says bars can't open until 1 p.m. on Sundays. So in the little town of Laurel this particular Sunday, 23 July 1989, things were quiet at The Pistol and at The Saloon. It was only 1.15 p.m. It was a little livelier at Cedarview Country Club, the nine-hole golf course just outside town. They were holding the Cedarview Invitational, and a bunch of the guys were in the lounge, watching television. It didn't matter that millions more around the world – in Bombay, Frankfurt, Brisbane, Tokyo, New York – were watching the same thing. This was theirs. Because some 4,500 miles and six hours to the east, on a parched golf course on the west coast of Scotland, a local boy was making good.

Remember that spindly, freckle-faced redhead who used to beat balls all day? Mark Calcavecchia? Well, at Royal Troon at 7.15 p.m. – 1.15 p.m. in Laurel – he dropped the final putt and became the 1989 Open champion. He did it like a champion, too. He could have double-bogeyed that last play-off hole and still won, but he didn't. He fired a five iron in there like it was the last shot he would ever hit, and he birdied. Back at Cedarview, they cheered. That Calcavecchia kid always was as bold as a pirate.

'There were about ten of us in the lounge, and I'll tell you – the tears came to our eyes,' said Neil Kluver, superintendent of schools in Randolph, fifteen miles west. 'I can remember when he was a kid, all he ever wanted to be was a golfer. When he finally hit the green at number five – that's 180 yards – he was only eleven years old. He was jumping up and down like it was Christmas. He was thirteen when he shot 32.'

Which was about when he played his last golf in Laurel.

Laurel, Nebraska, USA, population 1,035, situated in the north-east corner of the state, there in the Great Plains, where you can see a long way and drive a lot longer without coming across a soul. This is farm country – feed cattle, corn, beans. Back during the Second World War, Marjorie Christensen left Laurel to work in Washington, DC. John Calcavecchia, from New Jersey, was in the American Navy. They met, fell in love, and married. They moved back to Laurel after the war, and John, like so many GIs, had to find his way. He worked at a service station for a while, had a gravel pit, sold some insurance, and worked for an amusement machine company.

In 1973, when Mark was thirteen, the family moved to Florida. Some in Laurel say John wanted to move because of his failing health. (He died in 1985.) Others said that he realized from the time he helped found and build Cedarview that he had a real golfer on his hands and had to get the boy more playing time. They get some cattle-killing winters on the Great Plains. Mark didn't like Florida at first, until he discovered he could play golf all year round, even on Christmas Day. They think a lot of him in Laurel because he doesn't forget. He came home for a clinic and ceremony in 1988 – 'We didn't have to pay a nickel,' Kluver said – and they named the clubhouse entrance road 'Calcavecchia Drive'. Much of his dad is in that club, and also in his Open Championship.

'I know my dad is watching from up there, and he's happy,' Calcavecchia said. 'He gave me money when we didn't have money, he sent me places to play when we couldn't afford it. I owe so much to him.'

A fire-belly had won. 'He has a fire in his belly,' said Curtis Strange, who knows a brother when he sees one. As bold as Arnold Palmer ever was, they say: 'Kill the ball, find it, kill it again, and if they want this tournament, they're going to have to take it away from me.'

Calcavecchia, twenty-nine, was not an overnight success. He turned pro in 1981 and needed four cracks at the PGA Tour qualifying school before making it. He scored his first win in 1986, and – after two earlier victories in 1989 – the Open Championship made six.

But he came very close to not winning the Open.

'The baby is due any day, any minute,' Calcavecchia said. Sheryl was back home awaiting the arrival of their first child. He called immediately to tell her he had won the Open, but she had been watching on television. 'She was crying all over the place,' Calcavecchia said, 'And just as I was about to ask, she said, "No! I haven't had the baby yet!" '

Calcavecchia figured it was divine intervention that led him to win the Open Championship. 'A miracle from God is the only way to describe it,' he said. Not only Sheryl's insistence that he came to Royal Troon ('I have good vibes for you about the British Open,' she said); not only that forty-footer he holed to save par at number eleven; not only that crazy chip-in at number twelve, that hit the flagstick and dropped in for another saving par ('I was more embarrassed than anything else,' he said. 'I mean, how lucky can you get?'). And not only that wicked five iron out of the rough to six feet at number eighteen in the play-off, but most of all the co-operation of the baby.

'Because if I had got a phone call Saturday night that she had gone into labour,' Calcavecchia said, 'I'd have been on a plane out of here.'

On Sunday, Calcavecchia got up early and ran for three and a half miles. 'I didn't even realize I ran it,' he said. 'I was wondering how it would feel to win.' And then he knew.

At the start, there was no reason to believe Calcavecchia could win the Open. His track record on links courses was not convincing. In his two previous Opens, he tied for eleventh at Muirfield in 1987, and he missed the cut at Lytham in 1988. And this time he began the last round at nine under par and three strokes behind the leader, Wayne Grady. He slipped as far as five behind with ten holes to play. Calcavecchia didn't so much as sniff the lead until he birdied the eighteenth and tied Greg Norman at thirteen under par. Moments later, they were joined by Grady in a four-hole aggregate play-off. Norman birdied the first two holes, led by one, then self-destructed. He bogeyed the par-three seventeenth when he chipped too strong from the back fringe. Then at number eighteen, he went from bunker to bunker to out of bounds, and picked up. There was no point in playing on. Calcavecchia lay two just six feet in front of the pin after that shot from the rough. Grady was a little better off. Standing on the eighteenth too, he was two behind. He would need a miracle. But it was Calcavecchia's day for miracles. Calcavecchia parred the first hole, birdied the second from thirty-five feet, parred the seventeenth with two putts from fifty feet, and birdied the eighteenth from six feet after his last miracle. He was two-under-par 13 for the four holes, Grady was one-over 16, and Norman had no total score.

Back in Laurel, Nebraska, Mrs Marvalee Sudbeck, the librarian and town clerk (in the same building) remembers Calcavecchia as a typical little boy. 'He came in to check out books, mostly sports books,' she said. 'And I never had to scold him. He was very well-mannered. All the Calcavecchia children were very well-mannered. Their parents brought them up very well.'

Said her husband, Harold (an automotive repair-man): 'I remember Mark as a skinny, freckle-faced kid with shorts on, carrying his bag. His dad would drive a cart, and Mark would walk and beat the ball.'

Said Mrs Joyce Dalton, a family friend: 'Morning, afternoon, all the time – all golf. No football, no basketball, no baseball, just golf.'

Nobody had really heard of Calcavecchia until that name went up on the leader-board in the final round of the 1986 US Open at Shinnecock Hills. He had a 65. Not an eyelid fluttered. It happens all the time, someone catching lightning. The word on Calcavecchia was that he was a golf bum looking for a game, and if he couldn't find one, then he would pack somebody else's bag. A beachcomber who wandered on to a golf course. The truth was meaner than that.

True, there is a certain picaresque air about the guy. But he never was a golf bum. He wasn't mere-

Shortly after winning the Open Championship, Mark Calcavecchia was on the telephone to his wife Sheryl.

ly following the sun. He was trying to carve out a place for himself in it. And it will spoil the story, but we do not have an old caddy-to-riches tale here. Calcavecchia was never a caddy, unless doing an occasional favour qualifies a guy for that fraternity. Calcavecchia caddied for his pal, Ken Green, four times. Generally, it was because Green had qualified for a tournament and Calcavecchia had not. In the Las Vegas Classic once, Calcavecchia had to leave after the first round. About all he had left was his airline ticket.

The real source of the caddy myth was the 1986 Honda Classic. Calcavecchia was at home in Florida one day, soaking up the pleasure of a $19,000 mini-tour victory, when Green called for help from the Honda, not far away. His regular caddy, his sister Shelley, had broken her arm. This episode didn't come to light until he won the 1987 Honda Classic a year later. What a story: caddy one year, champion the next.

At Royal Troon, an American voice in the press corps put Calcavecchia on the spot. Calcavecchia was on the 1987 Ryder Cup team that lost in Europe's unprecedented second consecutive victory. This was a new Ryder Cup year, and Calcavecchia had drawn considerable attention with a certain remark he had made. Would you explain it, the American voice asked. Calcavecchia just laughed.

'I said I'd rather win the Ryder Cup than a major,' he said. 'That's because back then, I didn't think I had a chance to win a major, and I did think we have a hell of a chance to win the Ryder Cup.'

Calcavecchia keeps surprising himself, but not others. Take the square groves issues, golf's *cause célèbre* of the late 1980s. Critics say the square grooves in the clubface put so much spin on the ball, you can just about stop a shot on glass. This was technology, not skill, they said. As Jack Nicklaus put it, 'You could buy your game in the pro shop.' A lot of golfers were using square grooves. Calcavecchia merely was the best known. Said one supporting-cast American pro, who hadn't been doing much, 'If it weren't for square grooves, Calcavecchia would be working in a car wash.'

'Aw, did he really say that?' Calcavecchia said, chuckling. 'He probably was playing badly at the time.'

Nicklaus has delivered the majority opinion many times. 'Square grooves don't mean five cents to Mark,' Nicklaus said. 'He's a great player. He can win with anything.'

If nothing else, the grooves issue helped identify this Mark Calcavecchia, this guy with the auburn hair, freckles, and sad eyes. He is a friendly, open guy who bears no animosity to his critics; who would rather play golf than eat; a hamburger-and-fries kind of guy who likes to shoot pool and drink beer with the caddies; who listened to Sheryl's good sense and worked off the flab, and who needs, and returns, the warmth of family.

In his first big win, the 1987 Honda Classic, a Honda Accord was part of the prize. He gave it to his mother.

'I stuck with my old banger,' he said. It was a Chevrolet Camaro, vintage early 1980s, that got him around when he couldn't afford an air fare. 'It didn't have cruise control,' he said. 'It had a hole in the floor, where I put my foot.'

Finally, his day came early in 1989, when he won the Phoenix Open and two weeks later the Los Angeles Open. He bought a Porsche for himself and a BMW for Sheryl. 'About $180,000, total,' he said. Money didn't spoil him. He doesn't squander, but he doesn't stint either. His economic theory is a simple question: 'What's the good of money,' he asks, 'if you can't have any fun?'

There was some question how Calcavecchia would do in the play-off against Norman and Grady, because it wasn't long ago that he had some serious doubts about himself. 'I always wondered how I would do in a play-off,' he said. 'I always figured I would choke my guts out and make double-bogey on the first hole.' His test finally came in the 1987 Byron Nelson Classic. He lost to Fred Couples on the third hole, but not because he choked. His approach shot out of the rough cleared the green from 200 yards away. He had hit a nine iron.

He tested himself twice at Royal Troon, both times at number eighteen. In regulation, standing on the tee, he was a stroke behind Norman, who had finished with an inspired 64. 'I've got to make birdie or I'm history,' Calcavecchia said. He fired an eight iron 161 yards, to within four feet of the hole, and made his birdie for a 68. In the play-off, he didn't have a sword dangling over him at the eighteenth. Norman was in big trouble in the fairway bunker, and Grady was two strokes behind. Calcavecchia's tee shot had leaked to the right and was in the light rough, 201 yards from home. He could play it cozy and still win. But that wasn't part of the equation. There was only one question: Four iron or five iron? He took the five, and came away with a breathtaking, soaring shot that he could sense as much as see.

'It's a shot I'll never forget,' he said. 'I watched it, and I said I don't care where it ends up, because that's the best shot I've ever hit.'

The Open Championship, his first major victory, was riding on that one shot, and thousands were screaming and the world was watching. He didn't care.

Of the 29,818 yards this Open covered, only seven feet were left. Calcavecchia could play safe and two-putt for his par. But, of course, he didn't. A quick study, a confident stroke, a birdie-three, and the Open was his. It took him a while to realize it.

'My God!' Calcavecchia said. 'I've won the British Open.'

SUPREME SKILL
AND SPORTSMANSHIP

BY ALISTER NICOL

That Greg Norman is an extraordinarily gifted golfer has never been in question. A total of fifty-six victories worldwide, worth nearly $6 million in prize money since he turned professional in 1976, are more than sufficient testimony to his golfing skills.

His archetypal athletic good looks – broad-shouldered, thin-hipped, blond-maned – added to his confident personality equate to an irresistible marketing package which the rugged Australian and his management team have not been slow to exploit. He is a Madison Avenue dream figure. An annual sum of £6 million from his off-course businesses is not thought to be wildly inaccurate.

He was nicknamed 'Hollywood' when he first blazed on to the European Tour scene in the late 1970s. Greg's penchant for fast cars – and life in the fast lane as a bachelor – was such that he had to buy two Porsches. The first was too readily recognizable by the local constabulary around the leafy lanes of the Sunningdale district where he made his home, so he needed some camouflage.

Life has been good to Greg Norman, who nowadays likes to whisk round the exclusive enclave of North Palm Beach in his Rolls Royce, when he chooses to leave the Ferrari in the garage.

Married to a lovely wife, Laura, with two great kids, Morgan-Leigh (aged seven) and Gregory (four), a magnificent ocean-fronted mansion and with as much money as he will ever need to keep his family in the opulent manner to which they have been accustomed, the Great White Shark would appear to be cruising in calm waters.

If life has been good to him, the game of golf, to which he owes his comfort and riches, has been anything but. The golfing gods have dealt Gregory John Norman, still only aged thirty-four, a series of sickening blows, more than enough indeed to have

crushed a lesser man. The latest was hammered down on that famous mane on Sunday 23 July, at Royal Troon Golf Club on the final day of the 118th Open Championship.

Norman awoke that morning with the memory of a dream still fresh in a mind which some have suggested might just lack the intensity which has driven his friend Jack Nicklaus to a haul of twenty major titles. 'I dreamt I was going to start my last round with three birdie threes,' he revealed later. 'The dream was so vivid I could see every shot – the drives, the approaches, the putts.' The previous evening Norman had gone to bed in Troon's course-side hotel, the Highland Marine, languishing seven shots behind fellow Australian Wayne Grady after rounds of 69, 70 and 72. Before retiring he confided to friends that he needed a last round of 63 to have a chance of repeating his 1986 Open Championship success down the coast at Turnberry. That year the wind whipped across the Ailsa course's rough-lined fairways, which were as narrow as ribbons, and the cross winds made them look even slimmer. Some even claimed the course was unfair.

Norman ignored the obstacles on the second day, trusted in his own awesome game and self-belief, and strode on to the seventeenth tee facing a plausible eagle-birdie finish for a 60, only to take a 63. That round was the bedrock of Norman's victory, his only major title to date. An admiring Tom Watson, winner of five Open Championships, later paid high tribute to Norman's performance. He said, 'That is the greatest round ever played in a championship in which I was a competitor.'

Before his Turnberry triumph, Norman had led both that year's Masters and US Open after three rounds. He won neither. At Augusta, an inspired Jack Nicklaus came home in 30 for a 65 and a total of 279. Norman too was making a move. Successive birdies at the fourteenth, fifteenth, sixteenth and seventeenth saw him brew the Augusta excitement. He needed a par at the last to tie, a birdie to rob his life-long hero of a record sixth green jacket. The tee shot was good, leaving a four iron up the hill to the final green. Then, just as he had done two years previously at the seventy-second hole of the US Open at Winged Foot, Norman carved his four iron well right of the green. He bogeyed the hole, and the title went to Nicklaus. At least he did not have to wait until the following day as he had to do at Winged Foot, when Fuzzy Zoeller's 68 in a play-off was much too good for the Australian. Two majors within his grasp, two lost.

A few weeks later in that summer of 1986, Greg also led the US Open after three rounds at Shinnecock Hills on New York's Long Island. He carried a three-stroke advantage over Raymond Floyd to the first tee of the final round – and again lost. Then came Turnberry and Norman exorcized at least some of those demons conspiring against his bid for golfing immortality. On to the Inverness Country Club in Toledo, Ohio, for the US PGA Championship, the last of the year's major events. Again Greg was in front after three rounds. Again the victory was snatched away when Bob Tway holed a bunker shot beside the seventy-second green.

Each time, Norman was hurt, and badly hurt. Each time, he managed to hide that hurt. He disguised the agony with show after show of outstanding sportsmanship, courtesy and good will, when he would have been well excused for rearranging every item of furniture in view. He did not complain, he did not make excuses.

If Norman deserved medals for bravery after Winged Foot, Augusta, Shinnecock Hills and Inverness, he was surely due the Victoria Cross for what happened to him in the spring of 1987. Back at Augusta, he tied after seventy-two holes with old foe Severiano Ballesteros and local Georgia boy Larry Mize. In the fading light, the Spaniard three-putted his way out of the play-off. At the second extra hole, Augusta National's eleventh, Norman was on the green in two, with Mize 140 feet away to the

right, facing a difficult chip. He holed it. Norman's putt missed. For the fifth time in majors, and for the second time in a row, the Australian had been on the wrong end of outrageous fortune. Yet once again he displayed enormous fortitude. While Ballesteros was inconsolable and refusing to be interviewed by the world's golfing press, the ever-available Norman faced a barrage of questions with his enduring grace.

The following year at Augusta, Norman began the final round eleven strokes behind leader Sandy Lyle, one of his old friends and protagonists from his days on the European Tour. Even before the big Scot had started his day's work, Norman had the huge galleries yelling their delight and appreciation for his go-for-broke attacking skills. He went out in 30 and finally settled for a 64. That was good enough only for a share of fifth place, but it posted notice that the Great White Shark was back, that the wounds had healed and that he was still more than capable of beating the best – given a little help from Lady Luck.

On the eve of the US Open, played in 1988 at The Country Club in the Boston suburb of Brookline, Greg told me, 'I am ready. Fate is due me. I am sick and tired of being kicked in the groin.' He sounded sincere and he sounded confident. All he was doing, however, was tempting the fates that had consistently clobbered him with Mike Tyson-like blows. They struck again at Brookline. He selected a seven iron for his third shot to the long tenth off an innocuous-looking lie. A buried rock caught the club, damaged tendons in his left wrist and the tournament ended for him then and there, after only twenty-eight holes. He was forced to miss the Open Championship at Royal Lytham three weeks later.

The wrist still hurt when he arrived at Royal Troon less than fourteen months after the incident with the hidden rock. 'I take a couple of aspirin and some anti-inflammatory stuff every day because I still get pangs now and again. But this is the Open and I will not be pampering it even though the ground is hard,' he said typically. 'I will need surgery some time, but hopefully not until I am in my forties.'

That suspect wrist would not be the only thing to hurt by the end of the championship.

When Norman awoke from his dream he did indeed start with three birdies on Troon's fateful last day. Then he added three more in a row and by the time he had reached the turn he had taken only thirty strokes, ominously four of them at the short eighth. Measuring only 126 yards, the Postage Stamp is the shortest hole in championship golf.

'It's a real sucker-punch hole, though,' Norman had warned before a ball had been struck. In the last round he found a bunker and failed to get up and down. The Postage Stamp certainly suckered Greg, for the shot he dropped there robbed him of the 63 he reckoned he needed to win. He was right. His 64 was good enough only for the Open Championship's first play-off since 1975 and the first-ever to be decided over a four-hole format to be followed by sudden death if needed. His opponents were Wayne Grady and the brash and brave young Mark Calcavecchia.

What happened in that play-off is fully chronicled elsewhere, as are the events leading up to it, including Greg's 325-yard drive into a bunker at the fourth, and decisive, extra hole.

Surely to lose out after a final 64, after birdieing the first two play-off holes, after hitting 'too pure' a three iron to the third to drop a crucial shot, after clattering that colossal drive 325 yards into a bunker, then going out of bounds and not completing the hole . . .

Surely after all that he would go berserk. Surely that was too much even for Greg Norman to handle. Not a bit of it. His disappointment showed, of course. But there was no sign of bitterness, no hint of tantrums, no suggestion of recrimination, no sour grapes. Not even when Royal and Ancient secretary Michael Bonallack pointed out that Norman's last drive was the only one of the week to reach that bunker!

The 64 proved, as if proof were needed, that Greg Norman is indeed a player of extraordinary talent.

Much more importantly, however, his dignity and grace in defeat showed once more that Greg Norman is an exceptional man.

Mr Mark Benson of London, in a letter to *The Times*, wrote:

Whilst Greg Norman continues to grace the fairways of the world, sport, and more particularly, sportsmanship still has a chance.

His last round of 64 in this year's Open was awe-inspiring, as indeed was his drive on the final play-off hole which was still bounding along the fairway when it indicated right and finished in a bunker. Calcavecchia's shot was magical. Norman's was impossible. The outcome is now history. However, there is an image of those final moments which will linger for many years to come.

The way in which he handled this latest sequence of events was quite remarkable. With a warm smile on his face he was the first to congratulate Calcavecchia and without forgetting his countryman, Grady, the first to console a man who, like Norman, must have felt just a little disappointed.

At the end of the day Norman could have done no more. His supreme skill was matched by the ultimate in sportsmanship. This is what makes him a winner.

Greg Norman failed to win the 118th Open Championship at Royal Troon, but he made millions of friends. And surely to goodness the fiends who have kicked, gouged and scratched him for years will now turn elsewhere and leave the remarkable, exceptional Greg Norman alone.

He deserves a break – and a few major titles as well. How about starting with the 119th Open Championship at St Andrews in 1990? Or even Augusta?

Above, Greg Norman attempts a near-impossible bunker shot on the final play-off hole. Wayne Grady (below) had difficulties earlier, preventing him from winning the title outright.

COURAGE AND MORE COURAGE
BY JOHN HOPKINS

There's no more exciting sight in golf than Greg Norman on a charge. Head held high and back as straight as a guardsman's as he marches down the fairway; the sun touching his bleached hair; roars arising from different points of the course as word of his birdie barrage spreads; and, perhaps most memorable of all, his putter raised aloft in his outstretched left hand as he acknowledges yet another success. These are the images that remain in the mind's eye.

And on this Sunday, another day of blessed sunshine, Norman was in full flow, barging his way from far behind, passing players as easily as a sprinter would overtake a 1,500 metres runner. While warming up on the practice ground he had warned Nigel Mansell, the racing driver and an old friend, that he was going for it. 'I'm going to take my driver on every hole and to hell with it,' he said as Mansell watched drives soaring from Norman's clubface with the trajectory of a jet leaving nearby Prestwick. 'I'll either shoot 63 or 77.'

Norman's style is unique and thrilling. Seve Ballesteros is less predictable, sensational one minute, merely mortal the next. For the Spaniard it's all in a day's work when a sublimely-placed hole is followed by a tee shot forty yards off line. If unrelentless, error-free golf is the aim, then Nick Faldo is more accomplished than Norman. The tall Englishman gives the impression that there's nothing he would like better than to play eighteen holes of faultless golf.

Norman's powers of concentration are less than Curtis Strange's, he is only marginally longer than Ian Woosnam, and Sandy Lyle can be almost as brilliant, almost as long – and twice as bad. Nothing, however, matches the awesome sight of Norman at full stretch, booming out massive drives, shaping irons that never veer from the pin and then take that signature hop

backwards and stroking putts that drop down into the hole.

Other players break course records, set new targets in their own way. I suspect that Ben Crenshaw would love to sink eighteen birdie putts in as many holes – and if ever a man could, then he could. Norman doesn't want to sneak up on a course and defeat it when it's not looking or when it is defenceless. He wants to challenge it head-on and then wrestle it to the ground, jump on it with his spiked shoes and strangle it to within one inch of its life.

The way he began on the last day, 63 looked to be conservative. He single-putted the first three greens and was so close with his second shots on the first and third that one or other might have gone in for an eagle.

He reached the 557-yard fourth with a drive and a four iron and two putts maintained the sequence of birdies. Down went a fifteen-yarder on the short fifth and after the best chip of his life, he birdied the sixth hole, too. Six under after six holes, eleven under in all.

This was something special even by Norman's standards, for whom last-round charges are an integral part of a tournament. Often they have brought him close but not close enough – to within one stroke of winning at Augusta in three of the past four years, for instance. This time it seemed different. Now he was only one stroke behind Wayne Grady, his countryman, who hadn't yet teed off.

Norman couldn't master the Postage Stamp. A bogey there after missing the green was his only blemish all day and it temporarily dampened his inspiration. He didn't birdie the tenth and took out some of his frustration by lashing a drive so far down the aisle-like fairway of the eleventh, bordered by the railway on one side and grasping gorse on the other, that he needed only a sand wedge to reach the green. Another birdie.

The twelfth hole may have been the hole that turned an outstanding round into a great one. From all of forty-five feet, Norman calculated his putt precisely – five foot borrow and all. With its last, curling breath it fell into the hole. Now he was twelve under par. If he could steal two more birdies from Troon's secure-as-the-Bank-of-England last six holes, he would surely win the championship.

One came on the sixteenth, his eleventh in eighteen holes. He saved par by chipping in on the deadly seventeenth, holed for a four at the last to finish in 64, thirteen under par, eight shots better than he had started. It was as great a display of raw power and controlled aggression as has ever been seen on the final day of a major championship.

And yet it wasn't enough. He was destined to come up short in the three-man, four-hole play-off yet again. Just what goes wrong at the moment he's about to take that final step to the summit?

In 1986 when he won the Open at Turnberry, I was one of the many who predicted that Norman would go on and win more major championships. He was so big, strong, accurate, confident and determined, it seemed a matter of natural progression that he would take his share of the game's greatest titles. And yet thirty-six months and twelve major championships later, his total is still the same: one. A single major championship.

At different times in the meantime he has lost championships by indifferent shots of his own at the last hole, by a rival producing an unmatchable stroke on the final hole, by a flukish chip-in from fifty yards in a play-off. Truly, as Bob Verdi wrote in *Sports Illustrated* recently: 'It is possible that if he doesn't earn a Masters champion's green jacket soon, Greg Norman will opt for a strait-jacket instead . . . Is Norman over-anxious, overwrought, overdue, overrated?'

This time the denouement was the first three-man play-off over four holes in the championship's history, and it produced moments as thrilling as any. Norman can have no quibbles. He was beaten by a man who played better and equally courageously

for at least as long as he had. Not for nothing is Calcavecchia considered to be the most aggressive player on the US tour. That Sunday afternoon he showed aggression, skill and courage and it's worth noting in some detail on which holes he showed these qualities because it was so striking.

Almost every great round of golf contains moments of courage, brilliance and luck – and Calcavecchia's luck came at the twelfth hole. His five-iron second shot to the green hit a spectator and finished on a grassy ledge above and to the left of the green, twenty yards from the flag.

Calcavecchia could do no more than hack it out with his sand wedge and hope for the best. Imagine his amazement when it flew straight into the hole just as Lee Trevino's shot had disappeared improbably into the cup on the seventy-first hole of the 1972 Open at Muirfield. 'That kind of shot put a smile on my face,' remarked Calcavecchia.

From then on, it was courage, courage and more courage. Never once did he flinch from his task. On the sixteenth he used a one iron from the tee to position his drive perfectly on the 542-yard hole. It was near enough to Gnawys Burn for him to reach the green 275 yards away yet not so close that there was a danger of dribbling into what water was left after a ten-week drought.

Norman, earlier, had reached the green with a driver. Calcavecchia had to do the same. This wasn't the moment to be cautious. He smashed a stroke with his driver between the sentinel bunkers and thirty feet past the flag. It was a heroic shot, an act of controlled aggression. A birdie four came easily after such a brave shot.

The feisty American still had two crises to overcome. The first came on the green of the second play-off hole, the second hole. Wayne Grady had just missed his birdie. Norman held a one-stroke lead and lay closer to the flag than Calcavecchia, who had to sink his thirty-foot putt to pressurize Norman. If he missed, Norman would find it easier to hole his putt and take a two-stroke lead. Calcavecchia's putt turned in towards its target in its dying moments and toppled into the hole.

Calcavecchia's last test came on the eighteenth,

the final hole of the play-off. He hit a poor drive that rattled around among spectators standing on the right of the fairway. Grady's was straight and Norman's so far it rolled into a bunker 325 yards from the tee.

As he addressed his second shot, Calcavecchia was level with Norman, who had bogeyed the seventeenth, and two strokes ahead of Grady. He had 201 yards to the flag and hit a magnificent five iron that pulled up seven feet from the flag.

This was the stroke that won him the Open though he didn't know it yet. Grady was out of it and Norman, in a despairing effort to match Calcavecchia, tried to hoist a shot as far down the fairway as he could. The ball caught the lip of the bunker and rolled into another bunker. From here Norman's third shot flew over the green and out of bounds. It was another major championship he had not won, another big title gone.

Calcavecchia had triumphed because he had taken his luck when it was offered to him and he was brave enough to defeat each challenge as it arose. He produced the shot that mattered when it was most needed.

Norman, on the other hand, perhaps subconsciously mindful of the way that shots of his had drifted to the right on the last hole of the 1984 US Open and the 1985 Masters and of how he had left a five iron short of the eighteenth green in the 1989 Masters, couldn't do so.

In 1987 Tony Jacklin was asked how Norman's form had been affected by those two infamous hammer blows: Tway's chip-in from a bunker at the previous year's US PGA and Larry Mize's 140-foot chip-in at the Masters. 'Tell me that these sort of things don't affect you and I don't believe it,' Jacklin said. 'I should know, it happened to me at Muirfield in 1972.'

Jacklin, about to win his second Open, was shattered when Lee Trevino holed a lucky chip on the seventy-first green, causing a two-stroke swing. Trevino then went on to win.

'I was never the same afterwards,' Jacklin continued. 'Before Muirfield I couldn't believe anyone was better than me. After, I knew I wasn't the best in the world any longer.'

Jacklin had then paused for a moment as if he found it difficult to say what he wanted to, and this added to the dramatic effect. Then he said slowly and with difficulty, 'I'm sure Greg will win many more tournaments. But will he win majors? I don't know. I hope I'm wrong. I like him and admire what he has done for golf, but I don't know. I don't know.'

FINAL RESULTS

HOLE		1	2	3	4	5	6	7	8	9	10	11	12	13	14	15	16	17	18	
PAR		4	4	4	5	3	5	4	3	4	4	5	4	4	3	4	5	3	4	TOTAL
Mark Calcavecchia	Round 1	4	3	5	5	4	6	4	2	4	5	5	3	4	2	3	5	3	4	71
	Round 2	3	4	5	4	2	5	3	3	4	4	5	4	4	3	3	4	4	4	68
	Round 3	4	4	4	6	2	4	4	2	4	4	4	5	3	2	4	4	4	4	68
	Round 4	4	3	4	4	3	5	5	3	4	4	5	3	4	3	4	4	3	3	68-275
	PLAY-OFF	4	3	3	3															
Greg Norman	Round 1	4	5	4	4	3	4	4	3	3	4	4	4	4	3	4	5	3	4	69
	Round 2	3	4	4	4	4	5	4	3	5	4	4	4	5	3	4	4	2	4	70
	Round 3	4	4	4	4	3	4	3	4	4	4	6	5	4	3	4	5	2	5	72
	Round 4	3	3	3	4	2	4	4	4	4	4	4	3	4	3	4	4	3	4	64-275
	PLAY-OFF	3	3	4	x															
Wayne Grady	Round 1	4	4	4	4	3	4	3	2	4	4	4	4	4	3	4	5	4	4	68
	Round 2	4	3	4	5	2	5	3	2	5	3	4	4	4	3	4	5	3	4	67
	Round 3	4	4	4	5	3	5	4	3	4	3	4	4	4	3	4	4	3	4	69
	Round 4	3	4	4	4	2	5	4	3	5	4	5	3	4	4	4	5	4	4	71-275
	PLAY-OFF	4	4	4	4															
Tom Watson	Round 1	4	4	3	4	3	4	4	3	4	5	3	5	4	3	5	5	3	3	69
	Round 2	4	3	4	5	3	4	4	3	4	4	4	3	5	3	4	3	3	5	68
	Round 3	3	4	4	4	3	5	4	3	4	4	4	4	3	3	4	5	3	4	68
	Round 4	3	4	4	5	3	4	5	3	5	5	4	4	4	3	4	5	3	4	72-277
Jodie Mudd	Round 1	4	4	5	5	3	5	4	2	4	4	4	3	5	4	4	5	4	4	73
	Round 2	4	4	4	4	3	4	3	3	4	5	4	4	3	2	4	4	3	4	67
	Round 3	4	4	4	4	3	4	3	2	4	4	4	5	3	4	5	5	3	4	68
	Round 4	3	3	4	5	3	4	4	3	4	4	4	4	4	4	4	5	4	4	70-278
David Feherty	Round 1	4	4	4	4	4	4	3	4	4	4	5	4	5	2	4	4	4	4	71
	Round 2	3	4	4	4	2	4	4	2	4	4	4	4	3	3	4	6	3	5	67
	Round 3	4	3	4	4	3	5	4	3	4	4	4	3	5	3	4	5	3	4	69
	Round 4	3	4	4	5	4	4	4	3	4	4	4	5	4	4	5	4	3	4	72-279
Fred Couples	Round 1	4	4	4	4	2	4	4	4	4	4	4	4	4	3	4	4	3	4	68
	Round 2	4	4	5	5	3	5	5	3	4	4	4	3	3	2	4	5	3	5	71
	Round 3	4	3	4	4	3	5	4	2	4	4	4	4	3	4	4	4	3	5	68
	Round 4	4	5	4	6	3	6	3	4	5	5	5	3	4	3	3	4	2	3	72-279
Eduardo Romero	Round 1	4	4	4	3	3	4	4	3	4	4	4	4	5	3	4	4	3	4	68
	Round 2	5	5	4	5	3	4	4	2	4	4	4	3	4	3	4	5	3	4	70
	Round 3	5	4	5	5	3	6	4	3	5	3	5	5	4	3	4	4	3	4	75
	Round 4	4	4	4	5	3	4	3	2	4	4	4	3	4	3	4	5	3	4	67-280
Paul Azinger	Round 1	5	4	4	4	3	5	3	3	4	3	5	4	5	2	4	4	3	3	68
	Round 2	4	4	3	4	3	5	4	4	4	5	5	4	4	3	4	5	4	4	73
	Round 3	4	3	4	4	3	5	4	3	4	4	4	4	3	4	4	4	2	4	67
	Round 4	4	5	5	4	3	5	4	2	4	4	4	4	3	4	5	5	3	5	72-280
Payne Stewart	Round 1	4	5	3	4	3	4	4	3	4	4	5	4	5	3	5	5	3	4	72
	Round 2	4	3	4	4	3	3	4	3	4	4	4	4	4	2	5	4	3	3	65
	Round 3	4	4	4	4	3	5	4	3	3	4	4	4	4	4	4	5	2	4	69
	Round 4	4	4	3	5	3	4	4	4	6	4	4	4	3	4	6	4	3	5	74-280

RECORDS OF THE OPEN CHAMPIONSHIP

MOST VICTORIES
6, Harry Vardon, 1896-98-99-1903-11-14
5, James Braid, 1901-05-06-08-10; J.H. Taylor, 1894-95-1900-09-13; Peter Thomson, 1954-55-56-58-65; Tom Watson, 1975-77-80-82-83

MOST TIMES RUNNER-UP OR JOINT RUNNER-UP
7, Jack Nicklaus, 1964-67-68-72-76-77-79
6, J.H. Taylor, 1896-1904-05-06-07-14

OLDEST WINNER
Old Tom Morris, 46 years 99 days, 1867
Roberto de Vicenzo, 44 years 93 days, 1967

YOUNGEST WINNER
Young Tom Morris, 17 years 5 months 8 days, 1868
Willie Auchterlonie, 21 years 24 days, 1893
Severiano Ballesteros, 22 years 3 months 12 days, 1979

YOUNGEST AND OLDEST COMPETITOR
John Ball, 14 years, 1878
Gene Sarazen, 71 years 4 months 13 days, 1973

BIGGEST MARGIN OF VICTORY
13 strokes, Old Tom Morris, 1862
12 strokes, Young Tom Morris, 1870
8 strokes, J.H. Taylor, 1900 and 1913; James Braid, 1908
6 strokes, Bobby Jones, 1927; Walter Hagen, 1929; Arnold Palmer, 1962; Johnny Miller, 1976

LOWEST WINNING AGGREGATES
268 (68, 70, 65, 65), Tom Watson, Turnberry, 1977
271 (68, 70, 64, 69), Tom Watson, Muirfield, 1980
273 (67, 71, 70, 65), Severiano Ballesteros, Royal Lytham, 1988

LOWEST AGGREGATES BY RUNNER-UP
269 (68, 70, 65, 66), Jack Nicklaus, Turnberry, 1977
275 (68, 67, 71, 69), Lee Trevino, Muirfield, 1980
275 (70, 67, 69, 69), Nick Price, Royal Lytham, 1988

LOWEST AGGREGATE BY AN AMATEUR
283 (74, 70, 71, 68), Guy Wolstenholme, St Andrews, 1960

LOWEST INDIVIDUAL ROUND
63, Mark Hayes, second round, Turnberry, 1977; Isao Aoki, third round, Muirfield, 1980; Greg Norman, second round, Turnberry, 1986

LOWEST INDIVIDUAL ROUND BY AN AMATEUR
66, Frank Stranahan, fourth round, Troon, 1950

LOWEST FIRST ROUND
64, Craig Stadler, Royal Birkdale, 1983; Christy O'Connor Jr, Royal St George's, 1985; Rodger Davis, Muirfield, 1987

LOWEST SECOND ROUND
63, Mark Hayes, Turnberry, 1977; Greg Norman, Turnberry, 1986

LOWEST THIRD ROUND
63, Isao Aoki, Muirfield, 1980
64, Hubert Green and Tom Watson, Muirfield, 1980

LOWEST FOURTH ROUND
64, Graham Marsh, Royal Birkdale, 1983; Severiano Ballesteros, Turnberry, 1986; Greg Norman, Royal Troon, 1989

LOWEST FIRST 36 HOLES
132 (67, 65), Henry Cotton, Sandwich, 1934
133 (67, 66), Bobby Clampett, Royal Troon, 1982

LOWEST SECOND 36 HOLES
130 (65, 65), Tom Watson, Turnberry, 1977

LOWEST FIRST 54 HOLES
202 (68, 70, 64), Tom Watson, Muirfield, 1980
203 (68, 70, 65), Jack Nicklaus and Tom Watson, Turnberry, 1977

LOWEST FINAL 54 HOLES
200 (70, 65, 65), Tom Watson, Turnberry, 1977

LOWEST 9 HOLES
28, Denis Durnian, first 9, Royal Birkdale, 1983
29, Peter Thomson and Tom Haliburton, first 9, Royal Lytham, 1958; Tony Jacklin, first 9, St Andrews, 1970; Bill Longmuir, first 9, Royal Lytham, 1979; David J. Russell, first 9, Royal Lytham, 1988

CHAMPIONS IN THREE DECADES
Harry Vardon, 1896, 1903, 1911
J.H. Taylor, 1894, 1900, 1913
Gary Player, 1959, 1968, 1974

BIGGEST SPAN BETWEEN FIRST AND LAST VICTORIES
19 years, J.H. Taylor, 1894-1913
18 years, Harry Vardon, 1896-1914
15 years, Gary Player, 1959-74
14 years, Henry Cotton, 1934-48

SUCCESSIVE VICTORIES
4, Young Tom Morris, 1868-72. No championshp in 1871
3, Jamie Anderson, 1877-79; Bob Ferguson, 1880-82, Peter Thomson, 1954-56
2, Old Tom Morris, 1861-62; J.H. Taylor, 1894-95; Harry Vardon, 1898-99; James Braid, 1905-06; Bobby Jones, 1926-27; Walter Hagen, 1928-29; Bobby Locke, 1949-50; Arnold Palmer, 1961-62; Lee Trevino, 1971-72; Tom Watson, 1982-83

VICTORIES BY AMATEURS
3, Bobby Jones, 1926-27-30
2, Harold Hilton, 1892-97
1, John Ball, 1890
Roger Wethered lost a play-off in 1921

HIGHEST NUMBER OF TOP FIVE FINISHES
16, J.H. Taylor and Jack Nicklaus
15, Harry Vardon and James Braid

HIGHEST NUMBER OF ROUNDS UNDER 70
29, Jack Nicklaus
21, Tom Watson
18, Lee Trevino
16, Nick Faldo
15, Peter Thomson
14, Severiano Ballesteros
13, Gary Player
12, Bobby Locke, Arnold Palmer
11, Ben Crenshaw

OUTRIGHT LEADER AFTER EVERY ROUND
Willie Auchterlonie, 1893; J.H. Taylor, 1894 and 1900; James Braid, 1908; Ted Ray, 1912; Bobby Jones, 1927; Gene Sarazen, 1932; Henry Cotton, 1934; Tom Weiskopf, 1973

RECORD LEADS (SINCE 1892)
After 18 holes:
4 strokes, James Braid, 1908; Bobby Jones, 1927; Henry Cotton, 1934; Christy O'Connor Jr, 1985
After 36 holes:
9 strokes, Henry Cotton, 1934
After 54 holes:
10 strokes, Henry Cotton, 1934
7 strokes, Tony Lema, 1964
6 strokes, James Braid, 1908
5 strokes, Arnold Palmer, 1962; Bill Rogers, 1981

CHAMPIONS WITH EACH ROUND LOWER THAN PREVIOUS ONE
Jack White, 1904, Sandwich, 80, 75, 72, 69

James Braid, 1906, Muirfield, 77, 76, 74, 73
Ben Hogan, 1953, Carnoustie, 73, 71, 70, 68
Gary Player, 1959, Muirfield, 75, 71, 70, 68

CHAMPION WITH FOUR ROUNDS THE SAME
Densmore Shute, 1933, St Andrews, 73, 73, 73, 73 (excluding the play-off)

BIGGEST VARIATION BETWEEN ROUNDS OF A CHAMPION
14 strokes, Henry Cotton, 1934, second round 65, fourth round 79
11 strokes, Jack White, 1904, first round 80, fourth round 69; Greg Norman, 1986, first round 74, second round 63, third round 74

BIGGEST VARIATION BETWEEN TWO ROUNDS
17 strokes, Jack Nicklaus, 1981, first round 83, second round 66; Ian Baker-Finch, 1986, first round 86, second round 69

BEST COMEBACK BY CHAMPIONS
After 18 holes:
Harry Vardon, 1896, 11 strokes behind the leader
After 36 holes:
George Duncan, 1920, 13 strokes behind the leader
After 54 holes:
Jim Barnes, 1925, 5 strokes behind the leader
Of non-champions, Greg Norman, 1989, seven strokes behind the leader and lost in a play-off

CHAMPIONS WITH FOUR ROUNDS UNDER 70
None
Arnold Palmer, 1962, Tom Watson, 1977 and 1980, and Severiano Ballesteros, 1984, and Mark Calcavecchia, 1989, had three rounds under 70
Of non-champions, Phil Rodgers, 1963, Jack Nicklaus, 1977, Lee Trevino, 1980, Nick Faldo, 1984, Nick Price and Curtis Strange, 1988, Wayne Grady and Tom Watson, 1989, had three rounds under 70

BEST FINISHING ROUND BY A CHAMPION
65, Tom Watson, Turnberry, 1977; Severiano Ballesteros, Royal Lytham, 1988
66, Johnny Miller, Royal Birkdale, 1976

WORST FINISHING ROUND BY A CHAMPION SINCE 1920
79, Henry Cotton, Sandwich, 1934
78, Reg Whitcombe, Sandwich, 1938
77, Walter Hagen, Hoylake, 1924

WORST OPENING ROUND BY A CHAMPION SINCE 1919
80, George Duncan, Deal, 1920 (he also had a second round of 80)
77, Walter Hagen, Hoylake, 1924

BEST OPENING ROUND BY A CHAMPION
66, Peter Thomson, Royal Lytham, 1958
67, Henry Cotton, Sandwich, 1934; Tom Watson, Royal Birkdale, 1983; Severiano Ballesteros, Royal Lytham, 1988

BIGGEST RECOVERY IN 18 HOLES BY A CHAMPION

George Duncan, Deal, 1920, was 13 strokes behind the leader, Abe Mitchell, after 36 holes and level after 54

MOST APPEARANCES ON FINAL DAY (SINCE 1892)

30, J.H. Taylor
27, Harry Vardon, James Braid, Jack Nicklaus
26, Peter Thomson
24, Gary Player
23, Dai Rees
22, Henry Cotton

CHAMPIONSHIP WITH HIGHEST NUMBER OF ROUNDS UNDER 70

72, Royal Troon, 1989

CHAMPIONSHIP SINCE 1946 WITH THE FEWEST ROUNDS UNDER 70

St Andrews, 1946; Hoylake, 1947; Portrush, 1951; Hoylake, 1956; Carnoustie, 1968. All had only two rounds under 70

LONGEST COURSE

Carnoustie, 1968, 7252 yd (6631 m)

COURSES MOST OFTEN USED

Prestwick, 24 (but not since 1925); St Andrews, 23; Muirfield, 13; Sandwich, 11; Hoylake, 10; Royal Lytham, 8; Royal Troon, Musselburgh and Royal Birkdale, 6; Carnoustie, 5; Deal and Turnberry, 2; Royal Portrush and Prince's, 1

ATTENDANCE

Year	Attendance
1962	37,098
1963	24,585
1964	35,954
1965	32,927
1966	40,182
1967	29,880
1968	51,819
1969	46,001
1970	81,593
1971	70,076
1972	84,746
1973	78,810
1974	92,796
1975	85,258
1976	92,021
1977	87,615
1978	125,271
1979	134,501
1980	131,610
1981	111,987
1982	133,299
1983	142,892
1984	193,126
1985	141,619
1986	134,261
1987	139,189
1988	191,334
1989	160,639

PRIZE MONEY

Year	Total	First Prize
1860	nil	nil
1863	10	nil
1864	16	6
1876	20	20
1889	22	8
1891	28.50	10
1892	110	(Amateur winner)
1893	100	30
1910	125	50
1920	225	75
1927	275	100
1930	400	100
1931	500	100
1946	1,000	150
1949	1,700	300
1953	2,450	500
1954	3,500	750
1955	3,750	1,000
1958	4,850	1,000
1959	5,000	1,000
1960	7,000	1,250
1961	8,500	1,400
1963	8,500	1,500
1965	10,000	1,750
1966	15,000	2,100
1968	20,000	3,000
1969	30,000	4,250
1970	40,000	5,250
1971	45,000	5,500
1972	50,000	5,500
1975	75,000	7,500
1977	100,000	10,000
1978	125,000	12,500
1979	155,000	15,500
1980	200,000	25,000
1982	250,000	32,000
1983	300,000	40,000
1984	451,000	55,000
1985	530,000	65,000
1986	600,000	70,000
1987	650,000	75,000
1988	700,000	80,000
1989	750,000	80,000

Mark McNulty (left) and Mark James make their way round the course.

PAST RESULTS

* Denotes amateurs

1860 PRESTWICK

Willie Park, Musselburgh	55	59	60	174
Tom Morris Sr, Prestwick	58	59	59	176
Andrew Strath, St Andrews				180
Robert Andrew, Perth				191
George Brown, Blackheath				192
Charles Hunter, Prestwick St Nicholas				195

1861 PRESTWICK

Tom Morris Sr, Prestwick	54	56	53	163
Willie Park, Musselburgh	54	54	59	167
William Dow, Musselburgh	59	58	54	171
David Park, Musselburgh	58	57	57	172
Robert Andrew, Perth	58	61	56	175
Peter McEwan, Bruntsfield	56	60	62	178

1862 PRESTWICK

Tom Morris Sr, Prestwick	52	55	56	163
Willie Park, Musselburgh	59	59	58	176
Charles Hunter, Prestwick	60	60	58	178
William Dow, Musselburgh	60	58	63	181
* James Knight, Prestwick	62	61	63	186
* J.F. Johnston, Prestwick	64	69	75	208

1863 PRESTWICK

Willie Park, Musselburgh	56	54	58	168
Tom Morris Sr, Prestwick	56	58	56	170
David Park, Musselburgh	55	63	54	172
Andrew Strath, St Andrews	61	55	58	174
George Brown, St Andrews	58	61	57	176
Robert Andrew, Perth	62	57	59	178

1864 PRESTWICK

Tom Morris Sr, Prestwick	54	58	55	167
Andrew Strath, St Andrews	56	57	56	169
Robert Andrew, Perth	57	58	60	175
Willie Park, Musselburgh	55	67	55	177
William Dow, Musselburgh	56	58	67	181
William Strath, St Andrews	60	62	60	182

1865 PRESTWICK

Andrew Strath, St Andrews	55	54	53	162
Willie Park, Musselburgh	56	52	56	164
William Dow, Musselburgh				171
Robert Kirk, St Andrews	64	54	55	173
Tom Morris Sr, St Andrews	57	61	56	174
William Doleman, Glasgow	62	57	59	178

1866 PRESTWICK

Willie Park, Musselburgh	54	56	59	169
David Park, Musselburgh	58	57	56	171
Robert Andrew, Perth	58	59	59	176
Tom Morris Sr, St Andrews	61	58	59	178
Robert Kirk, St Andrews	60	62	58	180

Andrew Strath, Prestwick	61	61	60	182
* William Doleman, Glasgow	60	60	62	182

1867 PRESTWICK

Tom Morris, St Andrews	58	54	58	170
Willie Park, Musselburgh	58	56	58	172
Andrew Strath, St Andrews	61	57	56	174
Tom Morris Jr, St Andrews	58	59	58	175
Robert Kirk, St Andrews	57	60	60	177
* William Doleman, Glasgow	55	66	57	178

1868 PRESTWICK

Tom Morris Jr, St Andrews	50	55	52	157
Robert Andrew, Perth	53	54	52	159
Willie Park, Musselburgh	58	50	54	162
Robert Kirk, St Andrews	56	59	56	171
John Allen, Westward Ho!	54	52	63	172
Tom Morris St, St Andrews	56	62	58	176

1869 PRESTWICK

Tom Morris Jr, St Andrews	51	54	49	154
Tom Morris Sr, St Andrews	54	50	53	157
* S. Mure Fergusson, Royal and Ancient	57	54	54	165
Robert Kirk, St Andrews	53	58	57	168
David Strath, St Andrews	53	56	60	169
Jamie Anderson, St Andrews	60	56	57	173

1870 PRESTWICK

Tom Morris Jr, St Andrews	47	51	51	149
Bob Kirk, Royal Blackheath	52	52	57	161
David Strath, St Andrews	54	49	58	161
Tom Morris Sr, St Andrews	56	52	54	162
* William Doleman, Musselburgh	57	56	58	171
Willie Park, Musselburgh	60	55	58	173

1871 NO COMPETITION

1872 PRESTWICK

Tom Morris Jr, St Andrews	57	56	53	166
David Strath, St Andrews	56	52	61	169
* William Doleman, Musselburgh	63	60	54	177
Tom Morris Sr, St Andrews	62	60	57	179
David Park, Musselburgh	61	57	61	179
Charlie Hunter, Prestwick	60	60	69	189

1873 ST ANDREWS

Tom Kidd, St Andrews	91	88	179
Jamie Anderson, St Andrews	91	89	180
Tom Morris Jr, St Andrews	94	89	183
Bob Kirk, Royal Blackheath	91	92	183
David Strath, St Andrews	97	90	187
Walter Gourlay, St Andrews	92	96	188

1874 MUSSELBURGH

Mungo Park, Musselburgh	75	84	159
Tom Morris Jr, St Andrews	83	78	161
George Paxton, Musselburgh	80	82	162
Bob Martin, St Andrews	85	79	164
Jamie Anderson, St Andrews	82	83	165
David Park, Musselburgh	83	83	166
W. Thomson, Edinburgh	84	82	166

1875 PRESTWICK

Willie Park, Musselburgh	56	59	51	166
Bob Martin, St Andrews	56	58	54	168
Mungo Park, Musselburgh	59	57	55	171
Robert Ferguson, Musselburgh	58	56	58	172
James Rennie, St Andrews	61	59	57	177
David Strath, St Andrews	59	61	58	178

1876 ST ANDREWS

Bob Martin, St Andrews	86	90	176
David Strath, North Berwick	86	90	176
(Martin was awarded the title when Strath refused to play-off)			
Willie Park, Musselburgh	94	89	183
Tom Morris Sr, St Andrews	90	95	185
W. Thomson, Elie	90	95	185
Mungo Park, Musselburgh	95	90	185

1877 MUSSELBURGH

Jamie Anderson, St Andrews	40	42	37	41	160
Bob Pringle, Musselburgh	44	38	40	40	162
Bob Ferguson, Musselburgh	40	40	40	44	164
William Cosgrove, Musselburgh	41	39	44	40	164
David Strath, North Berwick	45	40	38	43	166
William Brown, Musselburgh	39	41	45	41	166

1878 PRESTWICK

Jamie Anderson, St Andrews	53	53	51	157
Bob Kirk, St Andrews	53	55	51	159
J.O.F. Morris, St Andrews	50	56	55	161
Bob Martin, St Andrews	57	53	55	165
* John Ball, Hoylake	53	57	55	165
Willie Park, Musselburgh	53	56	57	166
William Cosgrove, Musselburgh	53	56	55	166

1879 ST ANDREWS

Jamie Anderson, St Andrews	84	85	169
James Allan, Westward Ho!	88	84	172
Andrew Kirkaldy, St Andrews	86	86	172
George Paxton, Musselburgh			174
Tom Kidd, St Andrews			175
Bob Ferguson, Musselburgh			176

1880 MUSSELBURGH

Bob Ferguson, Musselburgh	81	81	162
Peter Paxton, Musselburgh	81	86	167
Ned Cosgrove, Musselburgh	82	86	168
George Paxton, Musselburgh	85	84	169
Bob Pringle, Musselburgh	90	79	169
David Brown, Musselburgh	86	83	169

1881 PRESTWICK

Bob Ferguson, Musselburgh	53	60	57	170
Jamie Anderson, St Andrews	57	60	56	173
Ned Cosgrove, Musselburgh	61	59	57	177
Bob Martin, St Andrews	57	62	59	178
Tom Morris Sr, St Andrews	58	65	58	181
Willie Campbell, Musselburgh	60	56	65	181
Willie Park Jr, Musselburgh	66	57	58	181

1882 ST ANDREWS

Bob Ferguson, Musselburgh	83	88	171
Willie Fernie, Dumfries	88	86	174
Jamie Anderson, St Andrews	87	88	175
John Kirkaldy, St Andrews	86	89	175
Bob Martin, St Andrews	89	86	175
* Fitz Boothby, St Andrews	86	89	175

1883 MUSSELBURGH

Willie Fernie, Dumfries	75	84	159
Bob Ferguson, Musselburgh	78	80	159
(Fernie won play-off 158 to 159)			
William Brown, Musselburgh	83	77	160
Bob Pringle, Musselburgh	79	82	161
Willie Campbell, Musselburgh	80	83	163
George Paxton, Musselburgh	80	83	163

1884 PRESTWICK

Jack Simpson, Carnoustie	78	82	160
David Rollan, Elie	81	83	164
Willie Fernie, Felixstowe	80	84	164
Willie Campbell, Musselburgh	84	85	169
Willie Park Jr, Musselburgh	86	83	169
Ben Sayers, North Berwick	83	87	170

1885 ST ANDREWS

Bob Martin, St Andrews	84	87	171
Archie Simpson, Carnoustie	83	89	172
David Ayton, St Andrews	89	84	173
Willie Fernie, Felixstowe	89	85	174
Willie Park Jr, Musselburgh	86	88	174
Bob Simpson, Carnoustie	85	89	174

1886 MUSSELBURGH

David Brown, Musselburgh	79	78	157
Willie Campbell, Musselburgh	78	81	159
Ben Campbell, Musselburgh	79	81	160
Archie Simpson, Carnoustie	82	79	161
Willie Park Jr, Musselburgh	84	77	161
Thomas Gossett, Musselburgh	82	79	161
Bob Ferguson, Musselburgh	82	79	161

1887 PRESTWICK

Willie Park Jr, Musselburgh	82	79	161
Bob Martin, St Andrews	81	81	162
Willie Campbell, Prestwick	77	87	164
* Johnny Laidlay, Honourable Company	86	80	166
Ben Sayers, North Berwick	83	85	168
Archie Simpson, Carnoustie	81	87	168

1888 ST ANDREWS

Jack Burns, Warwick	86	85	171
David Anderson Jr, St Andrews	86	86	172
Ben Sayers, North Berwick	85	87	172
Willie Campbell, Prestwick	84	90	174
* Leslie Balfour, Edinburgh	86	89	175
Andrew Kirkaldy, St Andrews	87	89	176
David Grant, North Berwick	88	88	176

1889 MUSSELBURGH

Willie Park Jr, Musselburgh	39	39	39	38	155
Andrew Kirkaldy, St Andrews	39	38	39	39	155
(Park won play-off 158 to 163)					
Ben Sayes, North Berwick	39	40	41	39	159
* Johnny Laidlay, Honourable Company	42	39	40	41	162
David Brown, Musselburgh	43	39	41	39	162
Willie Fernie, Troon	45	39	40	40	164

1890 PRESTWICK

* John Ball, Royal Liverpool	82	82	164
Willie Fernie, Troon	85	82	167
Archie Simpson, Carnoustie	85	82	167
Willie Park Jr, Musselburgh	90	80	170
Andrew Kirkaldy, St Andrews	81	89	170
* Horace Hutchinson, Royal North Devon	87	85	172

1891 ST ANDREWS

Hugh Kirkaldy, St Andrews	83	83	166
Willie Fernie, Troon	84	84	168
Andrew Kirkaldy, St Andrews	84	84	168
S. Mure Fergusson, Royal and Ancient	86	84	170
W.D. More, Chester	84	87	171
Willie Park Jr, Musselburgh	88	85	173

(From 1892 the competition was extended to 72 holes)

1892 MUIRFIELD

* Harold Hilton, Royal Liverpool	78	81	72	74	305
* John Ball Jr, Royal Liverpool	75	80	74	79	308
James Kirkaldy, St Andrews	77	83	73	75	308
Sandy Herd, Huddersfield	77	78	77	76	308
J. Kay, Seaton Carew	82	78	74	78	312
Ben Sayers, North Berwick	80	76	81	75	312

1893 PRESTWICK

Willie Auchterlonie, St Andrews	78	81	81	82	322
* Johnny Laidlay, Honourable Company	80	83	80	81	324
Sandy Herd, Huddersfield	82	81	78	84	325
Hugh Kirkaldy, St Andrews	83	79	82	82	326
Andrew Kirkaldy, St Andrews	85	82	82	77	326
J. Kay, Seaton Carew	81	81	80	85	327
R. Simpson, Carnoustie	81	81	80	85	327

1894 SANDWICH

J.H. Taylor, Winchester	84	80	81	81	326
Douglas Rolland, Limpsfield	86	79	84	82	331
Andrew Kirkaldy, St Andrews	86	79	83	84	332
A. Toogood, Eltham	84	85	82	82	333
Willie Fernie, Troon	84	84	86	80	334
Harry Vardon, Bury St Edmunds	86	86	82	80	334
Ben Sayers, North Berwick	85	81	84	84	334

1895 ST ANDREWS

J.H. Taylor, Winchester	86	78	80	78	322
Sandy Herd, Huddersfield	82	77	82	85	326
Andrew Kirkaldy, St Andrews	81	83	84	84	332
G. Pulford, Royal Liverpool	84	81	83	87	335
Archie Simpson, Aberdeen	88	85	78	85	336
Willie Fernie, Troon	86	79	86	86	337
David Brown, Malvern	81	89	83	84	337
David Anderson, Panmure	86	83	84	84	337

1896 MUIRFIELD

Harry Vardon, Ganton	83	78	78	77	316
J.H. Taylor, Winchester	77	78	81	80	316
(Vardon won play-off 157 to 161)					
* Freddie G. Tait, Black Watch	83	75	84	77	319
Willie Fernie, Troon	78	79	82	80	319
Sandy Herd, Huddersfield	72	84	79	85	320
James Braid, Romford	83	81	79	80	323

1897 HOYLAKE

* Harold H. Hilton, Royal Liverpool	80	75	84	75	314
James Braid, Romford	80	74	82	79	315
* Freddie G. Tait, Black Watch	79	79	80	79	317
G. Pulford, Royal Liverpool	80	79	79	79	317
Sandy Herd, Huddersfield	78	81	79	80	318
Harry Vardon, Ganton	84	80	80	76	320

1898 PRESTWICK

Harry Vardon, Ganton	79	75	77	76	307
Willie Park, Musselburgh	76	75	78	79	308
* Harold H. Hilton, Royal Liverpool	76	81	77	75	309
J.H. Taylor, Winchester	78	78	77	79	312
* Freddie G. Tait, Black Watch	81	77	75	82	315
D. Kinnell, Leven	80	77	79	80	316

1899 SANDWICH

Harry Vardon, Ganton	76	76	81	77	310
Jack White, Seaford	79	79	82	75	315
Andrew Kirkaldy, St Andrews	81	79	82	77	319
J.H. Taylor, Mid-Surrey	77	76	83	84	320
James Braid, Romford	78	78	83	84	322
Willie Fernie, Troon	79	83	82	78	322

1900 ST ANDREWS

J.H. Taylor, Mid-Surrey	79	77	78	75	309
Harry Vardon, Ganton	79	81	80	78	317
James Braid, Romford	82	81	80	79	322
Jack White, Seaford	80	81	82	80	323

| Willie Auchterlonie, St Andrews | 81 | 85 | 80 | 80 | 326 |
| Willie Park Jr, Musselburgh | 80 | 83 | 81 | 84 | 328 |

1901 MUIRFIELD

James Braid, Romford	79	76	74	80	309
Harry Vardon, Ganton	77	78	79	78	312
J.H. Taylor, Mid-Surrey	79	83	74	77	313
* Harold H. Hilton, Royal Liverpool	89	80	75	76	320
Sandy Herd, Huddersfield	87	81	81	76	325
Jack White, Seaford	82	82	80	82	326

1902 HOYLAKE

Sandy Herd, Huddersfield	77	76	73	81	307
Harry Vardon, South Herts	72	77	80	79	308
James Braid, Walton Heath	78	76	80	74	308
R. Maxwell, Honourable Company	79	77	79	74	309
Tom Vardon, Ilkley	80	76	78	79	313
J.H. Taylor, Mid-Surrey	81	76	77	80	314
D. Kinnell, Leven	78	80	79	77	314
*Harold H. Hilton, Royal Liverpool	79	76	81	78	314

1903 PRESTWICK

Harry Vardon, South Herts	73	77	72	78	300
Tom Vardon, Ilkley	76	81	75	74	306
Jack White, Sunningdale	77	78	74	79	308
Sandy Herd, Huddersfield	73	83	76	77	309
James Braid, Walton Heath	77	79	79	75	310
R. Thompson, North Berwick	83	78	77	76	314
A.H. Scott, Elie	77	77	83	77	314

1904 SANDWICH

Jack White, Sunningdale	80	75	72	69	296
James Braid, Walton Heath	77	80	69	71	297
J.H. Taylor, Mid-Surrey	77	78	74	68	297
Tom Vardon, Ilkley	77	77	75	72	301
Harry Vardon, South Herts	76	73	79	74	302
James Sherlock, Stoke Poges	83	71	78	77	309

1905 ST ANDREWS

James Braid, Walton Heath	81	78	78	81	318
J.H. Taylor, Mid-Surrey	80	85	78	80	323
R. Jones, Wimbledon Park	81	77	87	78	323
J. Kinnell, Purley Downs	82	79	82	81	324
Arnaud Massy, La Boulie	81	80	82	82	325
E. Gray, Littlehampton	82	81	84	78	325

1906 MUIRFIELD

James Braid, Walton Heath	77	76	74	73	300
J.H. Taylor, Mid-Surrey	77	72	75	80	304
Harry Vardon, South Herts	77	73	77	78	305
J. Graham Jr, Royal Liverpool	71	79	78	78	306
R. Jones, Wimbledon Park	74	78	73	83	308
Arnaud Massy, La Boulie	76	80	76	78	310

1907 HOYLAKE

| Arnaud Massy, La Boulie | 76 | 81 | 78 | 77 | 312 |
| J.H. Taylor, Mid-Surrey | 79 | 79 | 76 | 80 | 314 |

Tom Vardon, Sandwich	81	81	80	75	317
G. Pulford, Royal Liverpool	81	78	80	78	317
Ted Ray, Ganton	83	80	79	76	318
James Braid, Walton Heath	82	85	75	76	318

1908 PRESTWICK

James Braid, Walton Heath	70	72	77	72	291
Tom Ball, West Lancashire	76	73	76	74	299
Ted Ray, Ganton	79	71	75	76	301
Sandy Herd, Huddersfield	74	74	79	75	302
Harry Vardon, South Herts	79	78	74	75	306
D. Kinnell, Prestwick St Nicholas	75	73	80	78	306

1909 DEAL

J.H. Taylor, Mid-Surrey	74	73	74	74	295
James Braid, Walton Heath	79	73	73	74	299
Tom Ball, West Lancashire	74	75	76	76	301
C. Johns, Southdown	72	76	79	75	302
T.G. Renouf, Manchester	76	78	76	73	303
Ted Ray, Ganton	77	76	76	75	304

1910 ST ANDREWS

James Braid, Walton Heath	76	73	74	76	299
Sandy Herd, Huddersfield	78	74	75	76	303
George Duncan, Hanger Hill	73	77	71	83	304
Laurie Ayton, Bishops Stortford	78	76	75	77	306
Ted Ray, Ganton	76	77	74	81	308
W. Smith, Mexico	77	71	80	80	308
J. Robson, West Surrey	75	80	77	76	308

1911 SANDWICH

Harry Vardon, South Herts	74	74	75	80	303
Arnaud Massy, St Jean de Luz	75	78	74	76	303
(Play-off; Massy conceded at the 35th hole)					
Harold Hilton, Royal Liverpool	76	74	78	76	304
Sandy Herd, Coombe Hill	77	73	76	78	304
Ted Ray, Ganton	76	72	79	78	305
James Braid, Walton Heath	78	75	74	78	305
J.H. Taylor, Mid-Surrey	72	76	78	79	305

1912 MUIRFIELD

Ted Ray, Oxhey	71	73	76	75	295
Harry Vardon, South Herts	75	72	81	71	299
James Braid, Walton Heath	77	71	77	78	303
George Duncan, Hanger Hill	72	77	78	78	305
Laurie Ayton, Bishops Stortford	74	80	75	79	308
Sandy Herd, Coombe Hill	76	81	76	76	309

1913 HOYLAKE

J.H. Taylor, Mid-Surrey	73	75	77	79	304
Ted Ray, Oxhey	73	74	81	84	312
Harry Vardon, South Herts	79	75	79	80	313
M. Moran, Dollymount	76	74	89	74	313
Johnny J. McDermott, USA	75	80	77	83	315
T.G. Renouf, Manchester	75	78	84	78	315

1914 PRESTWICK

Harry Vardon, South Herts	73	77	78	78	306
J.H. Taylor, Mid-Surrey	74	78	74	83	309
H.B. Simpson, St Annes Old	77	80	78	75	310

Abe Mitchell, Sonning	76	78	79	79	312
Tom Williamson, Notts	75	79	79	79	312
R.G. Wilson, Croham Hurst	76	77	80	80	313

1920 DEAL

George Duncan, Hanger Hill	80	80	71	72	303
Sandy Herd, Coombe Hill	72	81	77	75	305
Ted Ray, Oxhey	72	83	78	73	306
Abe Mitchell, North Foreland	74	73	84	76	307
Len Holland, Northampton	80	78	71	79	308
Jim Barnes, USA	79	74	77	79	309

1921 ST ANDREWS

Jock Hutchison, USA	72	75	79	70	296
*Roger Wethered, Royal and Ancient	78	75	72	71	296
(Hutchison won play-off 150 to 159)					
T. Kerrigan, USA	74	80	72	72	298
Arthur G. Havers, West Lancs	76	74	77	72	299
George Duncan, Hanger Hill	74	75	78	74	301

1922 SANDWICH

Walter Hagen, USA	76	73	79	72	300
George Duncan, Hangar Hill	76	75	81	69	301
Jim Barnes, USA	75	76	77	73	301
Jock Hutchison, USA	79	74	73	76	302
Charles Whitcombe, Dorchester	77	79	72	75	303
J.H. Taylor, Mid-Surrey	73	78	76	77	304

1923 TROON

Arthur G. Havers, Coombe Hill	73	73	73	76	295
Walter Hagen, USA	76	71	74	75	296
Macdonald Smith, USA	80	73	69	75	297
Joe Kirkwood, Australia	72	79	69	78	298
Tom Fernie, Turnberry	73	78	74	75	300
George Duncan, Hanger Hill	79	75	74	74	302
Charles A. Whitcombe, Landsdowne	70	76	74	82	302

1924 HOYLAKE

Walter Hagen, USA	77	73	74	77	301
Ernest Whitcombe, Came Down	77	70	77	78	302
Macdonald Smith, USA	76	74	77	77	304
F. Ball, Langley Park	78	75	74	77	304
J.H. Taylor, Mid-Surrey	75	74	79	79	307
George Duncan, Hanger Hill	74	79	74	81	308
Aubrey Boomer, St Cloud, Paris	75	78	76	79	308

1925 PRESTWICK

Jim Barnes, USA	70	77	79	74	300
Archie Compston, North Manchester	76	75	75	75	301
Ted Ray, Oxhey	77	76	75	73	301
Macdonald Smith, USA	76	69	76	82	303
Abe Mitchell, Unattached	77	76	75	77	305

1926 ROYAL LYTHAM

| *Robert T. Jones Jr, USA | 72 | 72 | 73 | 74 | 291 |
| Al Watrous, USA | 71 | 75 | 69 | 78 | 293 |

Walter Hagen, USA	68	77	74	76	295
George von Elm, USA	75	72	76	72	295
Abe Mitchell, Unattached	78	78	72	71	299
T. Barber, Cavendish	77	73	78	71	299

1927 ST ANDREWS

*Robert T. Jones Jr, USA	68	72	73	72	285
Aubrey Boomer, St Cloud, Paris	76	70	73	72	291
Fred Robson, Cooden Beach	76	72	69	74	291
Joe Kirkwood, Australia	72	72	75	74	293
Ernest Whitcombe, Bournemouth	74	73	73	73	293
Charles Whitcombe, Crews Hill	74	76	71	75	296

1928 SANDWICH

Walter Hagen, USA	75	73	72	72	292
Gene Sarazen, USA	72	76	73	73	294
Archie Compston, Unattached	75	74	73	73	295
Percy Alliss, Berlin	75	76	75	72	298
Fred Robson, Cooden Beach	79	73	73	73	298
Jose Jurado, Argentina	74	71	76	80	301
Aubrey Boomer, St Cloud, Paris	79	73	77	72	301
Jim Barnes, USA	81	73	76	71	301

1929 MUIRFIELD

Walter Hagen, USA	75	67	75	75	292
John Farrell, USA	72	75	76	75	298
Leo Diegel, USA	71	69	82	77	299
Abe Mitchell, St Albans	72	72	78	78	300
Percy Alliss, Berlin	69	76	76	79	300
Bobby Cruickshank, USA	73	74	78	76	301

1930 HOYLAKE

*Robert T. Jones Jr, USA	70	72	74	75	291
Leo Diegel, USA	74	73	71	75	293
Macdonald Smith, USA	70	77	75	71	293
Fred Robson, Cooden Beach	71	72	78	75	296
Horton Smith, USA	72	73	78	73	296
Archie Compston, Coombe Hill	74	73	68	82	297
Jim Barnes, USA	71	77	72	77	297

1931 CARNOUSTIE

Tommy Armour, USA	73	75	77	71	296
Jose Jurado, Argentina	76	71	73	77	297
Percy Alliss, Berlin	74	78	73	73	298
Gene Sarazen, USA	74	76	75	73	298
Macdonald Smith, USA	75	77	71	76	299
John Farrell, USA	72	77	75	75	299

1932 PRINCE'S

Gene Sarazen, USA	70	69	70	74	283
Macdonald Smith, USA	71	76	71	70	288
Arthur G. Havers, Sandy Lodge	74	71	68	76	289
Charles Whitcombe, Crews Hill	71	73	73	75	292
Percy Alliss, Beaconsfield	71	71	78	72	292
Alf Padgham, Royal Ashdown Forest	76	72	74	70	292

1933 ST ANDREWS

Densmore Shute, USA	73	73	73	73	292
Craig Wood, USA	77	72	68	75	292
(Shute won play-off 149 to 154)					
Sid Easterbrook, Knowle	73	72	71	77	293
Gene Sarazen, USA	72	73	73	75	293
Leo Diegel, USA	75	70	71	77	293
Olin Dutra, USA	76	76	70	72	294

1934 SANDWICH

Henry Cotton, Waterloo, Belgium	67	65	72	79	283
Sid Brews, South Africa	76	71	70	71	288
Alf Padgham, Sundridge Park	71	70	75	74	290
Macdonald Smith, USA	77	71	72	72	292
Joe Kirkwood, USA	74	69	71	78	292
Marcel Dallemagne, France	71	73	71	77	292

1935 MUIRFIELD

Alf Perry, Leatherhead	69	75	67	72	283
Alf Padgham, Sundridge Park	70	72	74	71	287
Charles Whitcombe, Crews Hill	71	68	73	76	288
Bert Gadd, Brand Hall	72	75	71	71	289
Lawson Little, USA	75	71	74	69	289
Henry Picard, USA	72	73	72	75	292

1936 HOYLAKE

Alf Padgham, Sundridge Park	73	72	71	71	287
Jimmy Adams, Romford	71	73	71	73	288
Henry Cotton, Waterloo, Belgium	73	72	70	74	289
Marcel Dallemagne, France	73	72	75	69	289
Percy Alliss, Leeds Municipal	74	72	74	71	291
T. Green, Burnham Beeches	74	72	70	75	291
Gene Sarazen, USA	73	75	70	73	291

1937 CARNOUSTIE

Henry Cotton, Ashridge	74	72	73	71	290
Reg Whitcombe, Parkstone	72	70	74	76	292
Charles Lacey, USA	76	75	70	72	293
Charles Whitcombe, Crews Hill	73	71	74	76	294
Bryon Nelson, USA	75	76	71	74	296
Ed Dudley, USA	70	74	78	75	297

1938 SANDWICH

Reg Whitcombe, Parkstone	71	71	75	78	295
Jimmy Adams, Royal Liverpool	70	71	78	78	297
Henry Cotton, Ashridge	74	73	77	74	298
Alf Padgham, Sundridge Park	74	72	75	82	303
Jack Busson, Pannal	71	69	83	80	303
Richard Burton, Sale	71	69	78	85	303
Allan Dailey, Wanstead	73	72	80	78	303

1939 ST ANDREWS

Richard Burton, Sale	70	72	77	71	290
Johnny Bulla, USA	77	71	71	73	292
Johnny Fallon, Huddersfield	71	73	71	79	294
Bill Shankland, Temple Newsam	72	73	72	77	294
Alf Perry, Leatherhead	71	74	73	76	294

Reg Whitcombe, Parkstone	71	75	74	74	294
Sam King, Knole Park	74	72	75	73	294

1946 ST ANDREWS

Sam Snead, USA	71	70	74	75	290
Bobby Locke, South Africa	69	74	75	76	294
Johnny Bulla, USA	71	72	72	79	294
Charlie Ward, Little Aston	73	73	73	76	295
Henry Cotton, Royal Mid-Surrey	70	70	76	79	295
Dai Rees, Hindhead	75	67	73	80	295
Norman von Nida, Australia	70	76	74	75	295

1947 HOYLAKE

Fred Daly, Balmoral, Belfast	73	70	78	72	293
Reg Horne, Hendon	77	74	72	71	294
*Frank Stranahan, USA	71	79	72	72	294
Bill Shankland, Temple Newsam	76	74	75	70	295
Richard Burton, Coombe Hill	77	71	77	71	296
Charlie Ward, Little Aston	76	73	76	72	297
Sam King, Wildernesse	75	72	77	73	297
Arthur Lees, Dore and Totley	75	74	72	76	297
Johnny Bulla, USA	80	72	74	71	297
Henry Cotton, Royal Mid-Surrey	69	78	74	76	297
Norman von Nida, Australia	74	76	71	76	297

1948 MUIRFIELD

Henry Cotton, Royal Mid-Surrey	71	66	75	72	284
Fred Daly, Balmoral, Belfast	72	71	73	73	289
Norman von Nida, Australia	71	72	76	71	290
Roberto de Vicenzo, Argentina	70	73	72	75	290
Jack Hargreaves, Sutton Coldfield	76	68	73	73	290
Charlie Ward, Little Aston	69	72	75	74	290

1949 SANDWICH

Bobby Locke, South Africa	69	76	68	70	283
Harry Bradshaw, Kilcroney, Eire	68	77	68	70	283
(Locke won play-off 135 to 147)					
Roberto de Vicenzo, Argentina	68	75	73	69	285
Sam King, Knole Park	71	69	74	72	286
Charlie Ward, Little Aston	73	71	70	72	286
Arthur Lees, Dore and Totley	74	70	72	71	287
Max Faulkner, Royal Mid-Surrey	71	71	71	74	287

1950 TROON

Bobby Locke, South Africa	69	72	70	68	279
Roberto de Vicenzo, Argentina	72	71	68	70	281
Fred Daly, Balmoral, Belfast	75	72	69	66	282
Dai Rees, South Herts	71	68	72	71	282
E. Moore, South Africa	74	68	73	68	283
Max Faulkner, Royal Mid-Surrey	73	70	70	71	283

1951 ROYAL PORTRUSH

Max Faulkner, Unattached	71	70	70	74	285
Tony Cerda, Argentina	74	72	71	70	287
Charlie Ward, Little Aston	75	73	74	68	290
Fred Daly, Balmoral, Belfast	74	70	75	73	292
Jimmy Adams, Wentworth	68	77	75	72	292
Bobby Locke, South Africa	71	74	74	74	293

Bill Shankland, Temple Newsam	73	76	72	72	293
Norman Sutton, Leigh	73	70	74	76	293
Harry Weetman, Croham Hurst	73	71	75	74	293
Peter Thomson, Australia	70	75	73	75	293

1952 ROYAL LYTHAM

Bobby Locke, South Africa	69	71	74	73	287
Peter Thomson, Australia	68	73	77	70	288
Fred Daly, Balmoral, Belfast	67	69	77	76	289
Henry Cotton, Royal Mid-Surrey	75	74	74	71	294
Tony Cerda, Argentina	73	73	76	73	295
Sam King, Knole Park	71	74	74	76	295

1953 CARNOUSTIE

Ben Hogan, USA	73	71	70	68	282
*Frank Stranahan, USA	70	74	73	69	286
Dai Rees, South Herts	72	70	73	71	286
Peter Thomson, Australia	72	72	71	71	286
Tony Cerda, Argentina	75	71	69	71	286
Roberto de Vicenzo, Argentina	72	71	71	73	287

1954 ROYAL BIRKDALE

Peter Thomson, Australia	72	71	69	71	283
Sid Scott, Carlisle City	76	67	69	72	284
Dai Rees, South Herts	72	71	69	72	284
Bobby Locke, South Africa	74	71	69	70	284
Jimmy Adams, Royal Mid-Surrey	73	75	69	69	286
Tony Cerda, Argentina	71	71	73	71	286
J. Turnesa, USA	72	72	71	71	286

1955 ST ANDREWS

Peter Thomson, Australia	71	68	70	72	281
Johnny Fallon, Huddersfield	73	67	73	70	283
Frank Jowle, Edgbaston	70	71	69	74	284
Bobby Locke, South Africa	74	69	70	72	285
Tony Cerda, Argentina	73	71	71	71	286
Ken Bousfield, Coombe Hill	71	75	70	70	286
Harry Weetman, Croham Hurst	71	71	70	74	286
Bernard Hunt, Hartsbourne	70	71	74	71	286
Flory van Donck, Belgium	71	72	71	72	286

1956 HOYLAKE

Peter Thomson, Australia	70	70	72	74	286
Flory van Donck, Belgium	71	74	70	74	289
Roberto de Vicenzo, Argentina	71	70	79	70	290
Gary Player, South Africa	71	76	73	71	291
John Panton, Glenbervie	74	76	72	70	292
Henry Cotton, Temple	72	76	71	74	293
E. Bertolino, Argentina	69	72	76	76	293

1957 ST ANDREWS

Bobby Locke, South Africa	69	72	68	70	279
Peter Thomson, Australia	73	69	70	70	282
Eric Brown, Buchanan Castle	67	72	73	71	283
Angel Miguel, Spain	72	72	69	72	285
David Thomas, Sudbury	72	74	70	70	286
Tom Haliburton, Wentworth	72	73	68	73	286
*Dick Smith, Prestwick	71	72	72	71	286
Flory van Donck, Belgium	72	68	74	72	286

1958 ROYAL LYTHAM

Peter Thomson, Australia	66	72	67	73	278
David Thomson, Sudbury	70	68	69	71	278
(Thomson won play-off 139 to 143)					
Eric Brown, Buchanan Castle	73	70	65	71	279
Christy O'Connor, Killarney	67	68	73	71	279
Flory van Donck, Belgium	70	70	67	74	281
Leopoldo Ruiz, Argentina	71	65	72	73	281

1959 MUIRFIELD

Gary Player, South Africa	75	71	70	68	284
Flory van Donck, Belgium	70	70	73	73	286
Fred Bullock, Prestwick St Ninians	68	70	74	74	286
Sid Scott, Roehampton	73	70	73	71	287
Christy O'Connor, Royal Dublin	73	74	72	69	288
*Reid Jack, Dullatur	71	75	68	74	288
Sam King, Knole Park	70	74	68	76	288
John Panton, Glenbervie	72	72	71	73	288

1960 ST ANDREWS

Kel Nagle, Australia	69	67	71	71	278
Arnold Palmer, USA	70	71	70	68	279
Bernard Hunt, Hartsbourne	72	73	71	66	282
Harold Henning, South Africa	72	72	69	69	282
Roberto de Vicenzo, Argentina	67	67	75	73	282
*Guy Wolstenholme, Sunningdale	74	70	71	68	283

1961 ROYAL BIRKDALE

Arnold Palmer, USA	70	73	69	72	284
Dai Rees, South Herts	68	74	71	72	285
Christy O'Connor, Royal Dublin	71	77	67	73	288
Neil Coles, Coombe Hill	70	77	69	72	288
Eric Brown, Unattached	73	76	70	70	289
Kel Nagle, Australia	68	75	75	71	289

1962 TROON

Arnold Palmer, USA	71	69	67	69	276
Kel Nagle, Australia	71	71	70	70	282
Brian Huggett, Romford	75	71	74	69	289
Phil Rodgers, USA	75	70	72	72	289
Bob Charles, NZ	75	70	70	75	290
Sam Snead, USA	76	73	72	71	292
Peter Thomson, Australia	70	77	75	70	292

1963 ROYAL LYTHAM

Bob Charles, NZ	68	72	66	71	277
Phil Rodgers, USA	67	68	73	69	277
(Charles won play-off 140 to 148)					
Jack Nicklaus, USA	71	67	70	70	278
Kel Nagle, Australia	69	70	73	71	283
Peter Thomson, Australia	67	69	71	78	285
Christy O'Connor, Royal Dublin	74	68	76	68	286

1964 ST ANDREWS

Tony Lema, USA	73	68	68	70	279
Jack Nicklaus, USA	76	74	66	68	284
Roberto de Vicenzo, Argentina	76	72	70	67	285

Bernard Hunt, Hartsbourne	73	74	70	70	287
Bruce Devlin, Australia	72	72	73	73	290
Christy O'Connor, Royal Dublin	71	73	74	73	291
Harry Weetman, Selsdon Park	72	71	75	73	291

1965 ROYAL BIRKDALE

Peter Thomson, Australia	74	68	72	71	285
Christy O'Connor, Royal Dublin	69	73	74	71	287
Brian Huggett, Romford	73	68	76	70	287
Roberto de Vicenzo, Argentina	74	69	73	72	288
Kel Nagle, Australia	74	70	73	72	289
Tony Lema, USA	68	72	75	74	289
Bernard Hunt, Hartsbourne	74	74	70	71	289

1966 MUIRFIELD

Jack Nicklaus, USA	70	67	75	70	282
David Thomas, Dunham Forest	72	73	69	69	283
Doug Sanders, USA	71	70	72	70	283
Gary Player, South Africa	72	74	71	69	286
Bruce Devlin, Australia	73	69	74	70	286
Kel Nagle, Australia	72	68	76	70	286
Phil Rodgers, USA	74	66	70	76	286

1967 HOYLAKE

Roberto de Vicenzo, Argentina	70	71	67	70	278
Jack Nicklaus, USA	71	69	71	69	280
Clive Clark, Sunningdale	70	73	69	72	284
Gary Player, South Africa	72	71	67	74	284
Tony Jacklin, Potters Bar	73	69	73	70	285
Sebastian Miguel, Spain	72	74	68	72	286
Harold Henning, South Africa	74	70	71	71	286

1968 CARNOUSTIE

Gary Player, South Africa	74	71	71	73	289
Jack Nicklaus, USA	76	69	73	73	291
Bob Charles, NZ	72	72	71	76	291
Billy Casper, USA	72	68	74	78	292
Maurice Bembridge, Little Aston	71	75	73	74	293
Brian Barnes, Burnham & Berrow	70	74	80	71	295
Neil Coles, Coombe Hill	75	76	71	73	295
Gay Brewer, USA	74	73	72	76	295

1969 ROYAL LYTHAM

Tony Jacklin, Potters Bar	68	70	70	72	280
Bob Charles, NZ	66	69	75	72	282
Peter Thomson, Australia	71	70	70	72	283
Roberto de Vicenzo, Argentina	72	73	66	72	283
Christy O'Connor, Royal Dublin	71	65	74	74	284
Jack Nicklaus, USA	75	70	68	72	285
Davis Love Jr, USA	70	73	71	71	285

1970 ST ANDREWS

Jack Nicklaus, USA	68	69	73	73	283
Doug Sanders, USA	68	71	71	73	283
(Nicklaus won play-off 72 to 73)					
Harold Henning, South Africa	67	72	73	73	285
Lee Trevino, USA	68	68	72	77	285
Tony Jacklin, Potters Bar	67	70	73	76	286
Neil Coles, Coombe Hill	65	74	72	76	287

Peter Oosterhuis, Dulwich and Sydenham	73	69	69	76	287

1971 ROYAL BIRKDALE

Lee Trevino, USA	69	70	69	70	278
Lu Liang Huan, Taiwan	70	70	69	70	279
Tony Jacklin, Potters Bar	69	70	70	71	280
Craig de Foy, Coombe Hill	72	72	68	69	281
Jack Nicklaus, USA	71	71	72	69	283
Charles Coody, USA	74	71	70	68	283

1972 MUIRFIELD

Lee Trevino, USA	71	70	66	71	278
Jack Nicklaus, USA	70	72	71	66	279
Tony Jacklin, Potters Bar	69	72	67	72	280
Doug Sanders, USA	71	71	69	70	281
Brian Barnes, Fairway DR	71	72	69	71	283
Gary Player, South Africa	71	71	76	67	285

1973 TROON

Tom Weiskopf, USA	68	67	71	70	276
Neil Coles, Holiday Inns	71	72	70	66	279
Johnny Miller, USA	70	68	69	72	279
Jack Nicklaus, USA	69	70	76	65	280
Bert Yancey, USA	69	69	73	70	281
Peter Butler, Golf Domes	71	72	74	69	286

1974 ROYAL LYTHAM

Gary Player, South Africa	69	68	75	70	282
Peter Oosterhuis, Pacific Harbour	71	71	73	71	286
Jack Nicklaus, USA	74	72	70	71	287
Hubert Green, USA	71	74	72	71	288
Danny Edwards, USA	70	73	76	73	292
Lu Liang Huan, Taiwan	72	72	75	73	292

1975 CARNOUSTIE

Tom Watson, USA	71	67	69	72	279
Jack Newton, Australia	69	71	65	74	279
(Watson won play-off 71 to 72)					
Bobby Cole, South Africa	72	66	66	76	280
Jack Nicklaus, USA	69	71	68	72	280
Johnny Miller, USA	71	69	66	74	280
Graham Marsh, Australia	72	67	71	71	281

1976 ROYAL BIRKDALE

Johnny Miller, USA	72	68	73	66	279
Jack Nicklaus, USA	74	70	72	69	285
Severiano Ballesteros, Spain	69	69	73	74	285
Raymond Floyd, USA	76	67	73	70	286
Mark James, Burghley Park	76	72	74	66	288
Hubert Green, USA	72	70	78	68	288
Christy O'Connor Jr, Shannon	69	73	75	71	288
Tom Kite, USA	70	74	73	71	288
Tommy Horton, Royal Jersey	74	69	72	73	288

1977 TURNBERRY

Tom Watson, USA	68	70	65	65	268
Jack Nicklaus, USA	68	70	65	66	269

Hubert Green, USA	72	66	74	67	279
Lee Trevino, USA	68	70	72	70	280
Ben Crenshaw, USA	71	69	66	75	281
George Burns, USA	70	70	72	69	281

1978 ST ANDREWS

Jack Nicklaus, USA	71	72	69	69	281
Simon Owen, NZ	70	75	67	71	283
Ben Crenshaw, USA	70	69	73	71	283
Raymond Floyd, USA	69	75	71	68	283
Tom Kite, USA	72	69	72	70	283
Peter Oosterhuis, GB	72	70	69	73	284

1979 ROYAL LYTHAM

Severiano Ballesteros, Spain	73	65	75	70	283
Jack Nicklaus, USA	72	69	73	72	286
Ben Crenshaw, USA	72	71	72	71	286
Mark James, Burghley Park	76	69	69	73	287
Rodger Davis, Australia	75	70	70	73	288
Hale Irwin, USA	68	68	75	78	289

1980 MUIRFIELD

Tom Watson, USA	68	70	64	69	271
Lee Trevino, USA	68	67	71	69	275
Ben Crenshaw, USA	70	70	68	69	277
Jack Nicklaus, USA	73	67	71	69	280
Carl Mason, Unattached	72	69	70	69	280

1981 SANDWICH

Bill Rogers, USA	72	66	67	71	276
Bernhard Langer, Germany	73	67	70	70	280
Mark James, Otley	72	70	68	73	283
Raymond Floyd, USA	74	70	69	70	283
Sam Torrance, Caledonian Hotel	72	69	73	70	284
Bruce Leitzke, USA	76	69	71	69	285
Manuel Pinero, Spain	73	74	68	70	285

1982 TROON

Tom Watson, USA	69	71	74	70	284
Peter Oosterhuis, GB	74	67	74	70	285
Nick Price, South Africa	69	69	74	73	285
Nick Faldo, Glynwed Ltd	73	73	71	69	286
Des Smyth, EAL Tubes	70	69	74	73	286
Tom Purtzer, USA	76	66	75	69	286
Massy Kuramoto, Japan	71	73	71	71	286

1983 ROYAL BIRKDALE

Tom Watson, USA	67	68	70	70	275
Hale Irwin, USA	69	68	72	67	276
Andy Bean, USA	70	69	70	67	276
Graham Marsh, Australia	69	70	74	64	277
Lee Trevino, USA	69	66	73	70	278
Severiano Ballesteros, Spain	71	71	69	68	279
Harold Henning, South Africa	71	69	70	69	279

1984 ST ANDREWS

Severiano Ballesteros, Spain	69	68	70	69	276
Bernhard Langer, Germany	71	68	68	71	278
Tom Watson, USA	71	68	66	73	278

Fred Couples, USA	70	69	74	68	281
Lanny Wadkins, USA	70	69	73	69	281
Greg Norman, Australia	67	74	74	67	282
Nick Faldo, Glynwed Int.	69	68	76	69	282

1985 SANDWICH

Sandy Lyle, Scotland	68	71	73	70	282
Payne Stewart, USA	70	75	70	68	283
Jose Rivero, Spain	74	72	70	68	284
Christy O'Connor Jr, Ireland	64	76	72	72	284
Mark O'Meara, USA	70	72	70	.72	284
David Graham, Australia	68	71	70	75	284
Bernhard Langer, Germany	72	69	68	75	284

1986 TURNBERRY

Greg Norman, Australia	74	63	74	69	280
Gordon J. Brand, England	71	68	75	71	285
Bernhard Langer, Germany	72	70	76	68	286
Ian Woosnam, Wales	70	74	70	72	286
Nick Faldo, England	71	70	76	70	287

1987 MUIRFIELD

Nick Faldo, England	68	69	71	71	279
Rodger Davis, Australia	64	73	74	69	280
Paul Azinger, USA	68	68	71	73	280
Ben Crenshaw, USA	73	68	72	68	281
Payne Stewart, USA	71	66	72	72	281
David Frost, South Africa	70	68	70	74	282
Tom Watson, USA	69	69	71	74	283

1988 ROYAL LYTHAM

Severiano Ballesteros, Spain	67	71	70	65	273
Nick Price, Zimbabwe	70	67	69	69	275
Nick Faldo, England	71	69	68	71	279
Fred Couples, USA	73	69	71	68	281
Gary Koch, USA	71	72	70	68	281
Peter Senior, Australia	70	73	70	69	282

The

CARD OF THE
CHAMPIONSHIP COURSE
PAR & YARDAGE

Hole	Par	Yardage	Hole	Par	Yardage
1	4	362	10	4	437
2	4	391	11	5	481
3	4	381	12	4	432
4	5	556	13	4	468
5	3	210	14	3	180
6	5	577	15	4	457
7	4	400	16	5	542
8	3	126	17	3	223
9	4	419	18	4	425
Out	**36**	**3,422**	**In**	**36**	**3,645**
			Total	**72**	**7,067**